3D Typography

3D Typography
© 2010 by Jeanette Abbink & Emily CM Anderson

All 3D Typography © its respective creators.

Design by Jeanette Abbink (Rational Beauty)
and Emily CM Anderson
Typeset in LaPolice BP and FF Kievit
Cover and chapter photos by M−36
Captions written by Amber Bravo
Edited by Buzz Poole
Production managed by Christopher D Salyers

Every effort has been made to trace accurate owner-
ship of copyrighted text and visual materials used
in this book. Errors or omissions will be corrected
in subsequent editions, provided notification is sent
to the publisher.

Library of Congress Control # 2009939176
Printed and bound by Asia Pacific Offset, China
10 9 8 7 6 5 4 3 2 1 First edition

Mark Batty Publisher
36 West 37th Street,
Suite 409
New York, NY 10018
www.markbattypublisher.com

ISNB-13: 978-0-9841906-2-1

Distributed outside North America by:
Thames & Hudson LTD
181A High Holborn
London WC1V7QX
United Kingdom
Tel: 00 44 20 7845 5000
Fax: 00 44 20 7845 5055
www.thameshudson.co.uk

3DTypography

Jeanette Abbink &
Emily CM Anderson

Mark Batty Publisher, New York

Table of Contents

American Craft magazine:
Top to bottom
Let'em Eat Cake
August/September, 2008
This sugar and plexiglass title
treatment was created for an article
about a "Sugarcraft" exhibition
in Chicago. The letters are based
off of the magazine's typeface,
DTL Fleischmann.

Spiritual Revolutionary:
Lenore Tawney
February/March, 2008
This type treatment was created
for an article about Lenore Tawney,
an artist who radicalized the field
of fiber arts. The woven letter
type is based off a game created
by typographer Clotilde Olyff
(see pages 76–77, 125).

The Industrial Complex
April/May, 2008
For a profile of Marek Cecula,
an artist who breaks boundaries
between craft and design, industrial
designer Scott Newlin used rapid
protyping to create the title treatment in the magazine's typeface,
DTL Fleischmann.

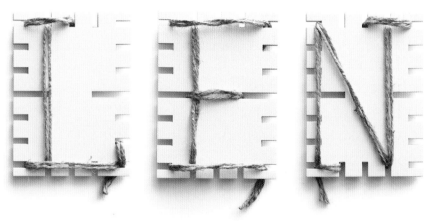

6

Preface

This book began, ironically enough, over traditional 2D type, when the two of us met to collaborate on a redesign of the venerable *American Craft* magazine. One of the longest continuously published periodicals in the country, the magazine was undergoing a tectonic shift in editorial focus, expanding its definition of "craft" while turning its gaze to a new generation of boundary-pushing artisans.

We grew excited by the possibility of creating a graphic environment that looked fresh and was organically connected to the work being depicted on the magazine's pages. Thus began our investigation into creating headlines from 3D letterforms that were rendered from such disparate materials as wood, sugar, clay, and thread.

Beautiful objects unto themselves, the hand-wrought pieces reflected upon the crafted letters they described in ways we found to be illuminating, soulful, and sometimes whimsical. As issue followed issue, we found ourselves foraging for inspiring examples of typographic projects from around the world to tack onto the wall, creating a dynamic backdrop to our brainstorming. As wall space grew scarce, we realized we had enough raw material for a larger project and compiled our burgeoning collection into this book.

As readers will discover, we haven't sacrificed all shreds of the endeavor's serendipitous nature. The chapter organization is somewhat improvisational, and—while chapter headings are a guide—it is our hope that the work can be appreciated from front to back, back to front, and by dipping into a page or two.

If you're anything like us, you may never look at letters in quite the same way—and may even be inspired to undertake a project of your own. As we learned, potential letterforms are everywhere, just waiting to be cut, carved, knitted, grown, spun, melted, molded, hammered, flown—and otherwise reclaimed.

Jeanette Abbink & Emily CM Anderson
New York City

Taking Type Back to the Human Side of the Screen

At the southern tip of Manhattan there's a building marked by thick, 12-foot-high letters, arranged in a semi-circle, beautifully illuminated in blue. "Staten Island Ferry"; that's what the steel mesh letters spell. The sign is a collaboration between the terminal's architect, Frederic Schwartz, who selected the exact shade of blue, and graphic designer Alexander Isley, who chose to use a typeface called Interstate, primarily for its "chunkiness." To me it's always felt like something more than a simple source of information. Because it sits in a part of Manhattan that is overstocked with big commemorative gestures—from the massive World War II East Coast Memorial in Battery Park to the Statue of Liberty out in the harbor—I tend to regard the Staten Island Ferry sign as a monument, a tribute to the power of the letterform.

I think a monument to type might be a good idea right about now. Type, long understood as a mechanism to transfer our thoughts and ideas to paper, is on the way out. Its function, its very essence is so profoundly in flux that our routine questions about type (Is it legible? Is it readable?) have given way to a new set of questions. What Gutenberg did over 550 years ago was invent a system in which the letters of the alphabet were cast in lead. For the centuries that followed not much really changed. Before you could print a book or a newspaper, you needed to have metal type. All that went away, beginning in the late 1940s, as cool phototypography gradually took the place of hot metal. And type as object receded even further into the past when digital typesetting took over in the 1980s. Now, type has gotten more ephemeral and less substantial. Type is set on one screen and read on another. It no longer exists in three dimensions, and only barely exists in two.

So the questions we now ask take us into the realm of the metaphysical. What is type exactly? Where does it come from? Does it exist in the real world or is it entirely made of phantom impulses?

If you think about it too hard, the current insubstantiality of type becomes a reminder that language itself is just a construct. And if you keep going, pretty soon the whole idea of meaning becomes intolerably iffy.

What's especially strange is that paper, never the strongest or most durable material, has begun to seem increasingly substantial as we depend on it less. In fact, it is precisely the un-tethering of type from paper that stirs the metaphysical pot. Until recently, everything that mattered was on paper: the Constitution, the Bible, *The New York Times*. Lately, the consequential stuff tends to arrive via iPhone text message. Sure, it's still Helvetica, and carries with it a whiff of that typeface's customary authority, but type today is a mere blip. It lives out its entire life cycle on the far side of the glass, intangible, remote, non-corporeal, elusive, transitory.

Back in 1994, I interviewed graphic designer Katherine McCoy at the moment she was leaving her post as the head of the design department at Cranbrook Academy of Art. We talked about the effect that the computer was having on her students and she mentioned a trend that she called "rematerialization." "There's a typeface a student designed a couple of years ago and he was just beginning to feel it was too much from the machine," she told me. "So he output each letter about six inches high, used those as the tracings, and cut wood blocks of the letters. Then he printed the wood blocks and scanned that type back into the computer with all the little blotches." McCoy added, "Two years ago, one of the degree show projects was all potato prints."

The hunger to rematerialize type, as McCoy described it, is a direct response to type's increasing dematerialization. As ink and paper typography flirts with obsolescence we've gotten fetishistic about the disappearing medium. For example, the current generation of e-readers, like Amazon's Kindle, involves a screen coated with an electroresponsive layer of tiny fragments, black and white, inside microcapsules floating in liquid. These particles obey the same binary pulses that drive all information technology. Pages of text are formed when positively charged white specks respond to a negative charge and negatively charged black specks respond to a positive charge. This coating, known as E-Ink, is strangely literal. The particles are actually manufactured from the same pigments that go into ink and paper, almost as if incorporating the essence of those traditional materials into a digital display will imbue the thing with bookishness. Like making aphrodisiacs from tiger penis or rhinoceros horn, it's a kind of voodoo.

In the interest of restoring tactility to the written language, artists and typographers sometimes practice what I think of as extreme rematerialization. Anna Garforth, a London-based illustrator, writes messages on walls in lush, green letterforms grown from living moss (see page 78). And Belgian typographer Clotilde Olyff creates alphabets from rocks she finds on the beach (see page 76). The pure physicality of her found alphabets recalls the heft of old school movable type, the chunks of lead, objects with dimensionality. Moss letters and rock letters are not intended to answer to questions of readability or legibility, but rather they are totemic objects intended to lure type back to the human side of the screen. When I see the photos of Garforth's moss or Olyff's rocks, I want to touch the type.

Type dematerialized to the point of being nothing is also type liberated from its utilitarian linguistic chores; it can also be anything and everything. It can be Rotterdam-based designer Thomas Voorn's "garment graffiti," messages in colorful, crinkly letters formed from old shirts (see page 136). Or, at its most literally, and excruciatingly, physical, type can be Amsterdam-based Thijs Verbeek's "typeface in skin," letterforms pulled from flesh and anchored by clothespins (see page 90). Underware, a Dutch graphic design studio, took the rematerialization of type a step further in a workshop they ran in Lausanne, Switzerland. They had students practice "Manual Pixelism," replicating digital pixels, the building blocks of electronic fonts, with physical objects. One group of students chose to substitute supermarket shopping carts for pixels and filled the store's parking lot with the words "dream on" (see page 128).

Sure, you can leaf through this book and simply admire the beauty and creativity of all the 3D type within. But you could also look at it as a group effort by artists, illustrators, and typographers to compensate for the growing insubstantiality of our written language, a compendium of ingenious ways the letters of the alphabet have been creatively rematerialized. The work represented in these pages suggests that there's a healthy tension between the worlds on either side of the screen, a constant give-and-take between the intangible and the tangible. The creators of 3D type have taken it upon themselves to restore to our words some of the heft and gravitas they had when Gutenberg got his start. Collectively, these artists, designers, and typographers strive to take the insubstantial and make it monumental.

Karrie Jacobs
New York City

Chapter 1

ATELIER PARIRI
EBON HEATH
KEETRA DEAN DIXON
AOYAMA HINA
BROCK DAVIS
ODED EZER
SHAZ MADANI
YULIA BRODSKAYA
JULIEN DE REPENTIGNY
CIARA PHELAN
SHARON PAZNER
DAVID ASPINALL
ALIDA ROSIE SAYER
OWEN GILDERSLEEVE
ARIS ZENONE
THORBJØRN ANKERSTJERNE
HUY VU
FONS HICKMAN
HANDMADEFONT
DANIELLA SPINAT
KEITH HANCOX
SONYA DYAKOVA

ATELIER PARIRI   3D TYPOGRAPHY

Untitled Paper Experiments Between Jérôme Corgier and Lara Captan

Paris-based Jérôme Corgier founded Atelier graphique Pariri in 2008. With the addition of Marie Holter in London, Lara Captan in Beirut, and Emilie Prat in Paris, the studio thrives on a multidisciplinary, multicultural exchange. Members work on their own individual projects, soliciting feedback and collaborative input from other members within the collective. The communication is largely remote, occurring via email and a collaborative blog called Jarajaja. The paper experiments are inspired by the challenges of communicating great distances and between Arabic and Latin letterforms. Captan and Corgier created a visual system called "topotypography" inspired by the codes and symbolism of cartography. The fruits of this experimentation extend to commissioned work as well, like the letterforms created for an instituational client on the following pages.

Question & Answer on page 212

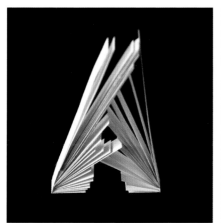

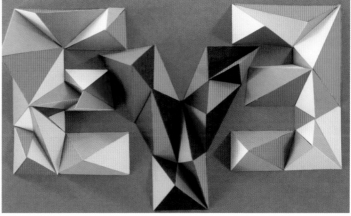

17

Stereotype

Living and working between
Brooklyn and Berlin, Ebon Heath's
interests are as diverse and far-
reaching as his transatlantic com-
mute. Heath founded (((stereotype))), a design studio focusing
on music packaging, magazine
layout, and fashion advertising.
In 2003, he turned his attention
to developing issue-based media
strategies for non-profits, NGOs,
and brands with his company
Cell Out. "Stereotype" is a self-
initiated series of typographic
sculptures that celebrate the letter's expressive quality beyond
the printed page or screen. The
series attempts to define a visual
language that has physicality
and presence—a body language.

EBON HEATH

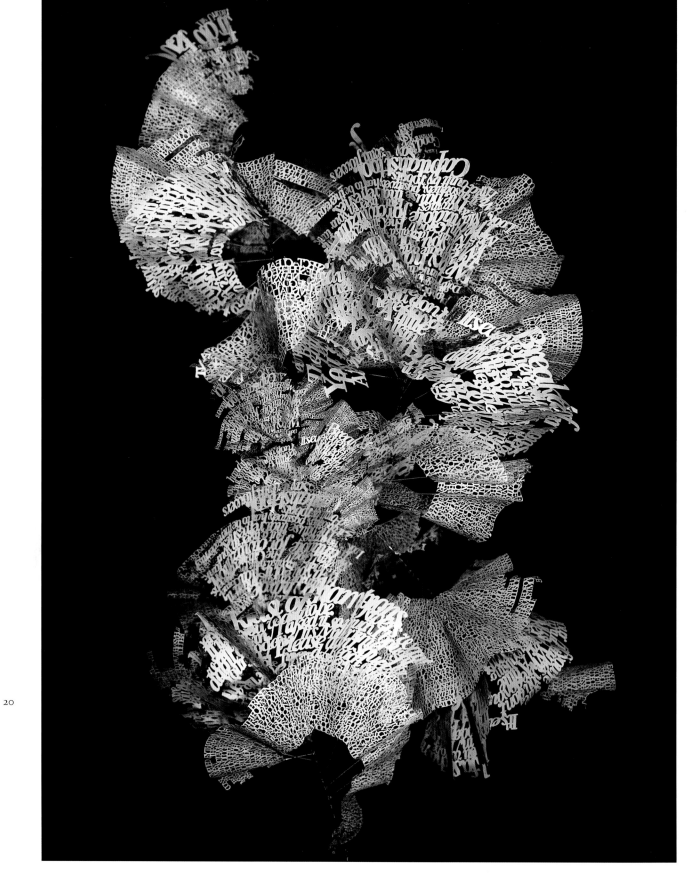

EBON HEATH

The Great Illusions

For this self-initiated piece, New York City-based designer and artist Keetra Dean Dixon (FromKeetra) did not work through a typical design process. "The poster has a slightly embarrassing back story," she explains. "I actually dreamt the general piece after my husband, JK Keller, and I had agreed secretly to get hitched...there was no sketching involved; the piece was complete in my head." Dixon wanted the poster to take a sardonic look at "themes in the human drama." The characters are at opposite ends of the spectrum. Both are asleep—one blindly in love and one blinded by "death." Behind each is written "the great romance" and "the great slumber," respectively. The props and type were made by hand.

21

KEETRA DEAN DIXON

Japanese paper artist Aoyama
Hina creates super fine lacy-paper-
cuttings with a pair of scissors.
For Sentences, Hina weaves pas-
sages into organic webs of text
and flourish. The pieces are labor-
intensive—a short work will take
up to five hours to make, while
a long work could take up to three
months. Hina, who lives and works
in Ferney Volaire, France, says of
her work: "I don't follow tradition,
but I am trying to create a mix-
ture of the traditional and modern
styles, to produce my own world
through this technique."

23

AOYAMA HINA

Currently serving as the creative director at Carmichael Lynch, artist and musician Brock Davis's creative interests span music, drawing, graphic design, and writing. "I don't think I've ever actually said 'keep it real' to anyone," says Davis, "but I had the phrase stuck in my head, and I thought it'd be interesting to portray it as a contradiction." For Shredded, Davis disrupted letterforms by cutting strips systematically through the type. In doing this, he illicits a tension between the cleanliness of sans serif typography and the idiosyncracy of craft.

BROCK DAVIS

ODED EZER

I♥Milton (opposite page)
Ketubah
After presenting at the Typo Berlin conference, renowned Israeli typographer Oded Ezer resolved to make more work in English: "I saw the enthusiasm of the audience when I showed a single piece in English, while the Hebrew designs were unreadable to most." Thus began a series of homages to non-Israeli designers, like Milton Glaser. For I♥Milton, Ezer manipulated Glaser's iconic logo. "Glaser's design is simple and direct," explains Ezer, "and I felt it would still be recognizable even if I made it more complicated." For Ketubah (a Jewish prenuptial agreement) Ezer used a different typeface—Zapfino, Goudy Old Style, Shoken, Caslon, and Beit Hillel—for each language appearing in this multilingual document.

Question & Answer on page 214

ODED EZER

Artic Paper Campaign Proposal
A graduate of Central Saint
Martins College of Art, Iranian-
born Shaz Madani's proposal
for Artic Paper bridges the gap
between high-quality creativity
and environmental thinking.
By using positive and negative cut
letterforms, the London-based
designer created images that em-
body the company's ethos through
visual puns and 3D composition.
Like Artic's product, the result
is both craft-oriented and refined.

Power of Imagination,
Papergraphic Illustration for
the Imaginary Foundation
Yulia Brodskaya's broad interest
in textile painting, origami,
and collage led her to pursue a
Master's in Graphic Communication
at the University of Hertfordshire.
Since graduating, the Russian-
born, UK-based Brodskaya has
developed a professional practice
that incorporates typography and
paper to create highly detailed
handmade craft objects for clients
like *The New York Times,* Hermes,
Starbucks, and Nokia.

29

YULIA BRODSKAYA

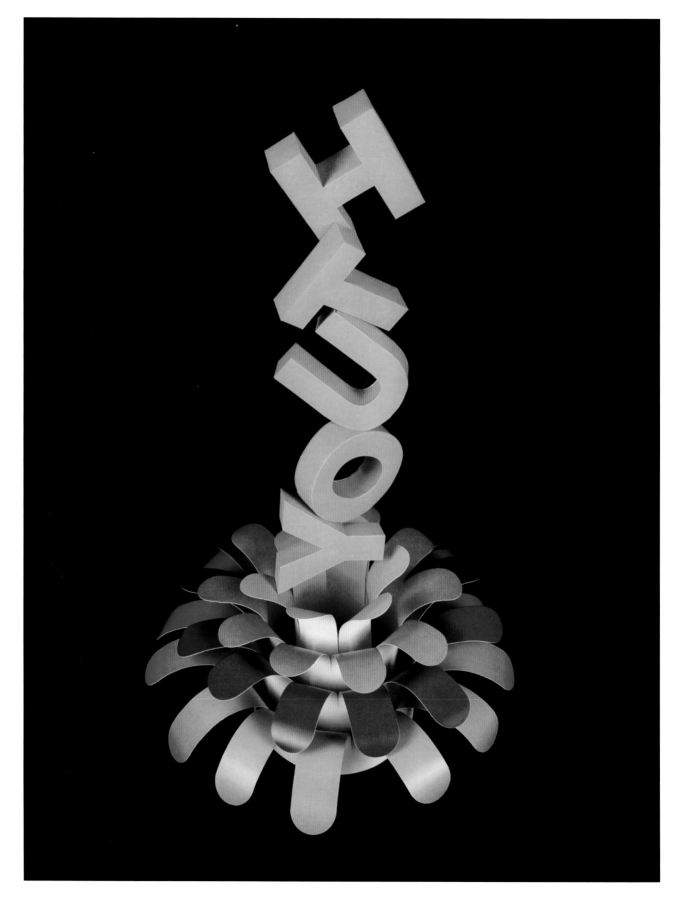

Self-Initiated Experiments with Cardboard Type

Julien De Repentigny is a graphic designer and art director living and working in Montreal. His work ranges from corporate branding to self-initiated projects like the cardboard type experiments shown here. For Fountain of Youth, (opposite page) De Repentigny was inspired to illustrate a concept through literal form. Milk is an experiment in cardboard packaging and communication, in which the content of the product is represented in the simplest way, both through word and image. The packaging is the same dimension as a 2 liter carton of milk. For Happiness, De Repentigny made an illustration montage constructed entirely out of cardboard and candy; it represents, ironically, the loss of innocence and happiness. His Helvetica package design (next page), is simply that: packaging made from Helvetica letterforms.

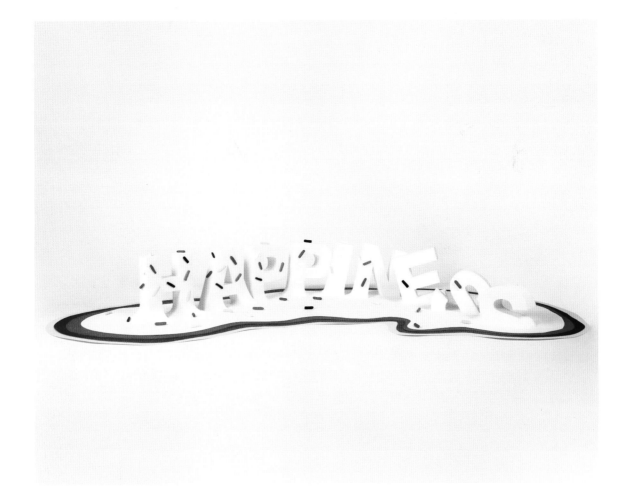

31

JULIEN DE REPENTIGNY

Graduate Invite
For the University of Brighton's
School of Historical and Critical
Studies 2007 Graduate Show
Invite, London-based designer
Ciara Phelan stacked and staggered
hand-cut paper to create a vibrant,
multilayered composition. Phelan
often experiments with illustrative
and geometric elements to create
her graphic work.

CIARA PHELAN

Love, 4 A's, and Shalom
Having studied architecture in both Jerusalem and Paris, Tel-Aviv-based artist Sharon Pazner's interest in volume comes as no surprise. Pazner works with what she calls "mirror letters"—3D letters that she makes using their mirror images, reflected in different directions. Love refers to Robert Indiana's iconic sculpture; 4 A's is more of a formal study in which the angle of the A's sits adjacently to form an arch. Shalom is made from cut paper reminiscent of Jerusalem's old city wall. As Pazner explains, "I designed letters... I see as harmonious and delicate, contrasting the idea of a wall."

Shredding Is All About the Details
London-based graphic designer David Aspinall's typographic experiment came from a series of work that explored ways of creating 3D letterforms from 2D materials: "I like the idea of embossing type in a different way and came to a fairly logical conclusion that I could do this by shredding the paper. I also liked the thought that the design would be partially out of my control." Each strip of paper had a different number of up and down folds, which resulted in a spontaneous pattern along the bottom edge of the paper.

35

DAVID ASPINALL

ALIDA ROSIE SAYER

Untitled

Glasgow School of Art graduate Alida Rosie Sayer is a designer working in illustration, 3D design, and animation. Her work often draws upon traditional craft techniques, such as paper cutting and letterpress printing, but is executed with an eye toward digital processes. For this self-initiated project, Sayer set about visualizing time using quotations from Kurt Vonnegut's *Slaughterhouse Five*. The text is rendered using multiple layers of hand-cut letterpress prints and sheets of drafting film suspended from wall-mounted rods. (Project continues on page 196.)

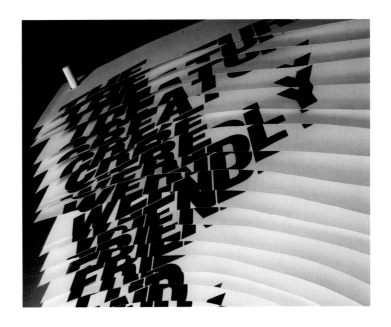

ALIDA ROSIE SAYER

Designer and illustrator Owen Gildersleeve grew up in the small village of Wedmore in the South West of England, where he spent most of his time running around fields and building tree houses. Gildersleeve now lives and works in London, where he is one quarter of the Evening Tweed design collective. For Ithaqua, one of two pieces Gildersleeve created for Mike Perry's "Cut It Out" exhibition held at the Open Space gallery in Beacon, New York, the designer hand-cut a paper image of Ithaqua, a yeti with glowing red eyes, and type reading: "God of the Cold White Silence."

Lectures dans La Ville
(Readings in Town)
Switzerland-based graphic designer
Aris Zenone works primarily
in the cultural and social sector,
doing editorial, book, and poster
design as well as type design.
For the program and poster,
Zenone set about illustrating the
power of words with 3D letters
cut from colored paper and pieces
of shopping bags. "The idea was
to bring a third dimension of
passion, color, dreams, words,
literature, poetry, quietness, into
a given day," says Zenone.

ARIS ZENONE

Specialten 21
Danish designer Thorbjørn
Ankerstjerne graduated in 2007
from Central Saint Martins with a
BA in graphic design. As a freelance
designer, he enjoys working across
a broad range of media from video,
installations, and sculpture to
conventional graphic design.
In addition, he also runs *FILE*
magazine. Ankerstjerne was asked
to art direct *Specialten 21* magazine, which featured hand-folded
paper letters throughout. The type
is constructed out of 2,500 paper
units, with each letter measuring
nearly four feet high.

40

Void

Form and counterform are essential to the legibility of a typeface. Huy Vu's <u>Void</u> was designed with the intention of adding mass into counterforms. After rendering his typeface with construction paper, Vu began experimenting with legibility. Using strobe lights modified with snoots and grids, he used light to hide and reveal the facets of his typeface. A New York City native, Vu recently returned to his hometown after graduating from Rhode Island School of Design with an MFA in graphic design; prior to that, he studied biology at Carleton College.

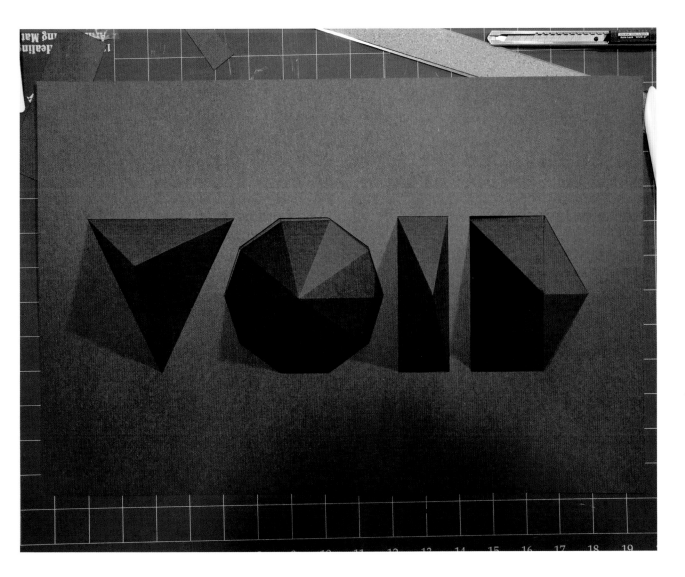

41

M23 Karton, Typeface Made From Cardbord Boxes
Fons Hickmann designed a complete typeset of 40 characters with the cardboard boxes he used to move from Vienna, Austria, to Berlin, Germany. Hickmann and Gesine Grotrian-Steinweg run the Berlin-based studio, Fons Hickmann m23, which focuses on corporate design, book and poster design, magazine design, and digital media. The work is at once conceptual and analytical without ever sacrificing a sense of humor.

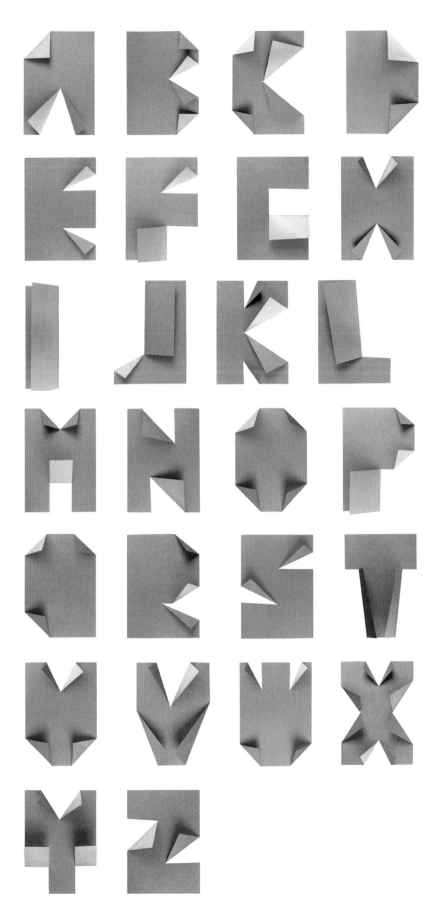

A4

Brothers Maksim Loginov and Vladmir Loginov are the master-minds behind HandMadeFont, a studio specializing in non-traditional fonts, which the duo post and sell on their website. For their self-initiated project, the Loginovs used size A4 paper sheets and scissors to create a blocky, faceted alphabet. When the brothers aren't designing letterforms, they are still working together as designers at AGE McCann, a large advertising firm in Tallinn, Estonia.

43

For her self-initiated typeface, Daniella Spinat reduced each letterform into folded paper: "I was trying to work in the spirit of Josef Albers's typography reductions, and I liked the idea of creating the forms out of light and shadow—using this essential element of photography to draw out form. I also restricted myself to a letter-size paper proportion, though, rightly or wrongly, I broke this rule with the 'M.'" Spinat graduated from Yale School of Art with a degree in graphic design; she currently lives and works in Seattle.

44

Dazzle Camouflage

Keith Hancox is a graphic designer living and working in the UK. For this self-initiated project Hancox employed Razzle Dazzle, Norman Wilkinson's camouflage painting method, which was used extensively on ships during World War I. Razzle Dazzle camouflage does not conceal, but rather makes it difficult to discern distance and speed. Hancox applied this method to various 3D forms so that, when viewed from a distance, the forms spell out the acronym HMS.

KEITH HANCOX

Paper Alphabet
Sonya Dyakova, Associate Art
Director of Phaidon Press, London,
designed Paper Alphabet for
Sculpture Today, a comprehensive
survey of contemporary sculpture.
Dyakova set out to develop a set
of sculptural letterforms by cutting and folding a flat sheet of paper. Considerable effort went into
crafting and arranging the letterforms, each one playfully varying
in shape and size, while its depth
remained constant. Legibility
is largely dependent on the side
from which one views the type.

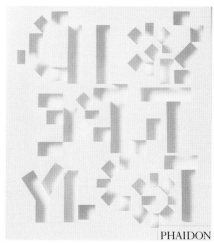

46

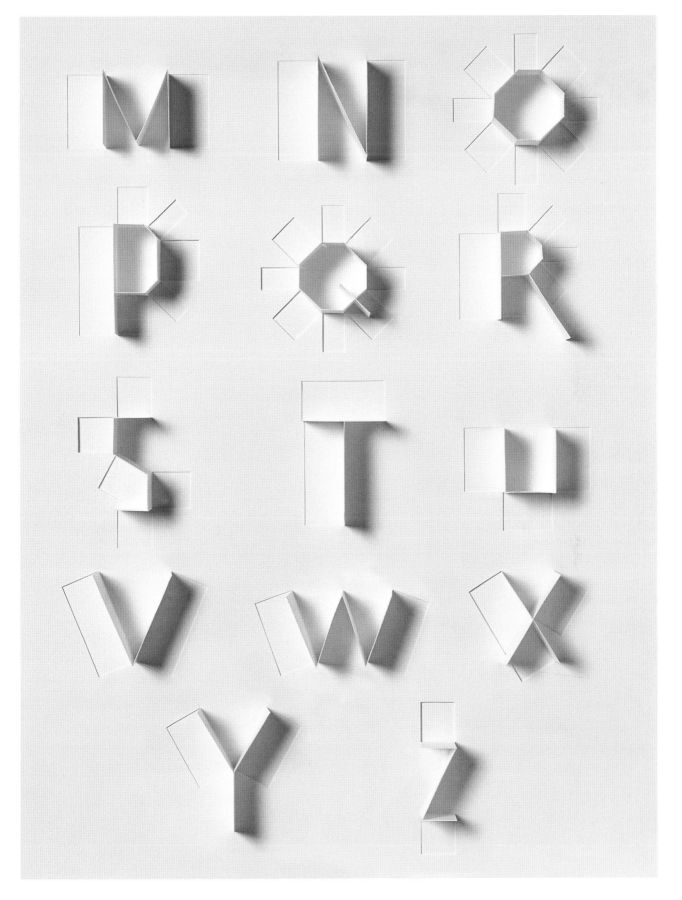

SONYA DYAKOVA

Chapter 2

Zigzag Zombie

The Zigzag Zombie type workshop was conceived by Underware for Dutch Design Week 2007 in Eindhoven, the Netherlands. The brief was to create continuous lettering out of a single material like rolls of paper, tape, thin metal, or cardboard, for example. Once a visual style was established, designers set out to make their mark on the town. Collaborators included: Eric de Haas aka The Broken Headlines in cooperation with Freek Lomme, Remco van de Caats and Erik Sjouerman, HeyHeyHey, The little league, Onomatopee, GreyTones, Hell shop, De Daily Whatever, Helden van de Heidelberg, Roots, Volle Kracht, EDHV, WordWide, Other things, Erosie aka the very special mystery guest, & Etropolis.

Question & Answer on page 221

Rubies Record Cover Design
Artist and musician Simone Rubi
used continuous strips of paper
to design the cover art for her band
Rubies's single, "I Feel Electric."
In addition to touring throughout
Europe and America, Rubi is
currently designing the opening
credits for two films, using paper,
thread, fabric, and light.

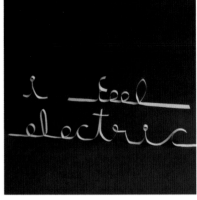

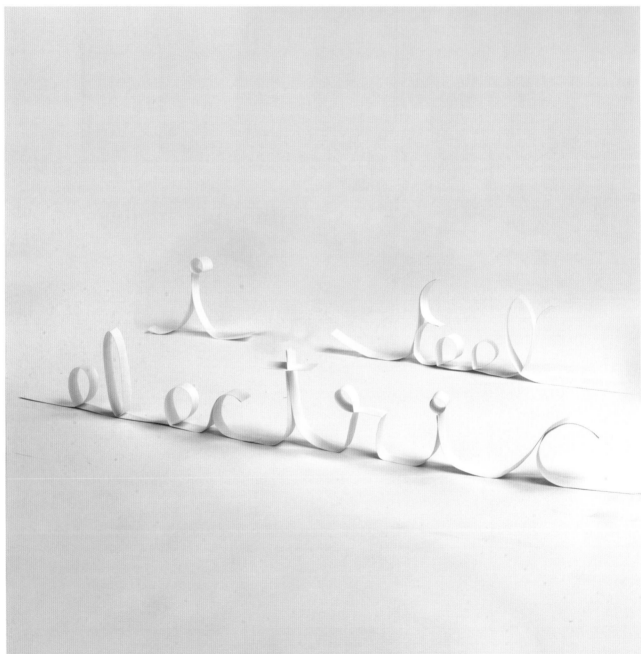

SIMONE RUBI

Each morning Moscow-based graphic designer Svetlana Sebyakina wakes to create a piece of typographic artwork. She explains, "This work is my attitude toward the morning, to quote Joseph Brodsky 'a man is what he loves. That's why he loves it: because he is part of it.'" These works are representative of Sebyakina's everyday passion. (Project continues on page 132.)

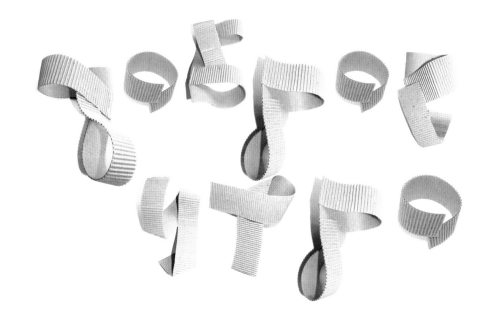

53

SVETLANA SEBYAKINA

UK-based graphic designers Miles
Gould and Joe Luxton conceived
this installation for The Karlheinz
Stockhausen Festival, Klang.
Inspired by the composer's methods
of controlled chance in serial
composition, Gould created an
interactive dream weaving
installation, in which participants
could actively weave patterns
through a structured grid.

For an issue of *NRC Next* magazine,
the Dutch design firm Autobahn
was asked to provide illustrative
typography to accompany feature
articles. The designers used gadgets
and cords to spell out the headline
for the article, "Vrij van stand-
by," which explores the possibility
of unplugging in a digital age.
Question & Answer on page 210

55

FANNY DUCOMMUN

Switzerland-based graphic designer Fanny Ducommun created this woven typeface with yarn and cardstock. The piece was produced in conjunction with a Lizzie Finn workshop at the ECAL/Ecole cantonale d'art de Lausanne from which Ducommun graduated with a degree in graphic design.

FANNY DUCOMMUN

Twilight, Gravity, and Our Many Impossible Things
New York City-based artist and designer Mario Hugo used a continuous string of silk and cotton thread to hand-embroider Twilight, Gravity, and Our Many Impossible Things into an organic hemp canvas. The gaps and idiosyncrasies in the text are a natural result of this needle and thread experiment, which he produced for The Mill, a visual effects company based in London, New York, and Los Angeles.

58

Graphic designers Rhonda
Drakeford and Harry Woodrow
founded Multistorey in 1997,
after graduating from Central Saint
Martins College. For an exhbition
exploring the cross-pollination
between contemporary architecture
and fashion design, the London-
based designers used transparent
plastic pins and metallic thread
to draw display typography.

PARALLEL PRACTICES IN
FASHION AND ARCHITECTURE

24th APRIL - 10th AUGUST

59

Danke Schön and Live Free or Die!
For <u>Danke Schön</u> New York City-
based designer and artist JK Keller
used ornate gold ribbon and his
Paulette typeface to write out the
words "thank you" in German.
For <u>Live Free or Die</u> he painstakingly wrapped caution tape around
a chain link fence to deliver
a message that is threatening yet
oddly affirmative.

60

A Bored Person is a Boring Person
London-based graphic designer
David Marsh created this experimental typography using two
continuous pieces of electrical wire
fixed to a white wall. The black
and red wires interchangeably form
the exterior and interior lines
in type, creating a dynamic tension.

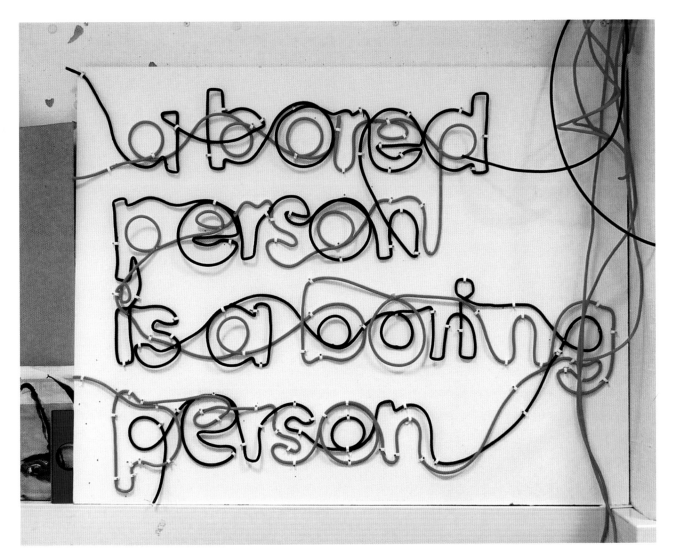

DAVID MARSH

Delight, Moments, Exchange, and In Vivo in Vitro
(Clockwise from top)
For over a decade Vienna-based artist Brigitte Kowanz has used light and language to create refracted multilayered artwork. Using materials like steel, neon, and mirrors her pieces evoke a playful, dynamic spirit.

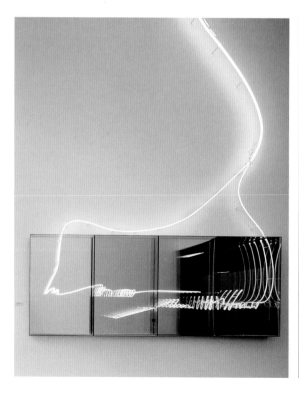

62

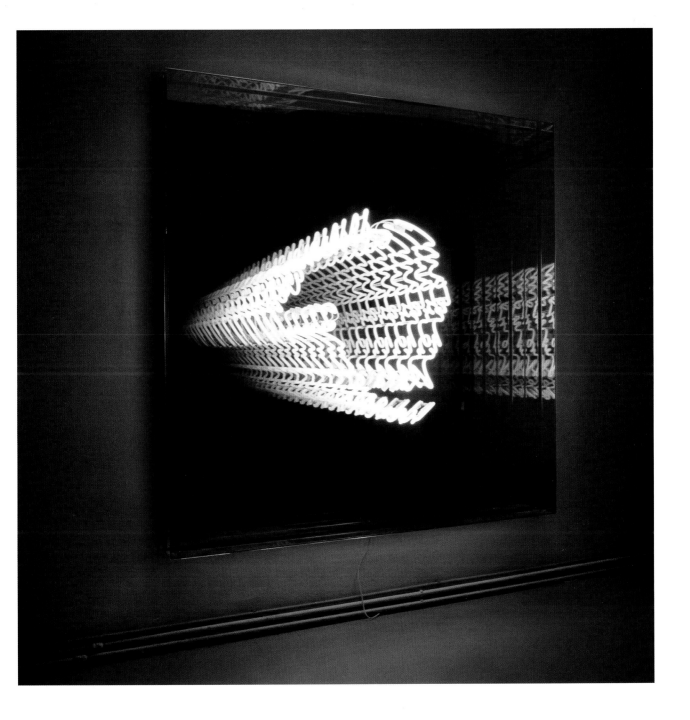

BRIGITTE KOWANZ

Nail Grid
For this self-initiated project, London-based designer Matthew Croft constructed an isometric nail grid around which he wrapped string and lace to produce typographic illustration. The grid allows for improvisation while maintaining a cohesive visual language.

Buenos Aires-based graphic
designer and illustrator Pablo
Alfieri created this concert
flyer for the Argentinean band
The Ovnis, using plasticine and
black acrylic. A graduate of the
University of Buenos Aires, Alfieri
worked for various design firms
throughout the city before founding his studio, Playful, in 2008.

65

PABLO ALFIERI

French-born, London-based graphic designer Amandine Alessandra's Lewis Carroll recontextualizes the author's quotation: "I have proved by actual trial that a letter, that takes an hour to write, takes only about 3 minutes to read!" Carroll's sentiment is represented tautologically: the words (or "letters") have taken hours to write/weave across the gate; it is Alessandra's hope that they won't take more than 3 minutes to read.

66

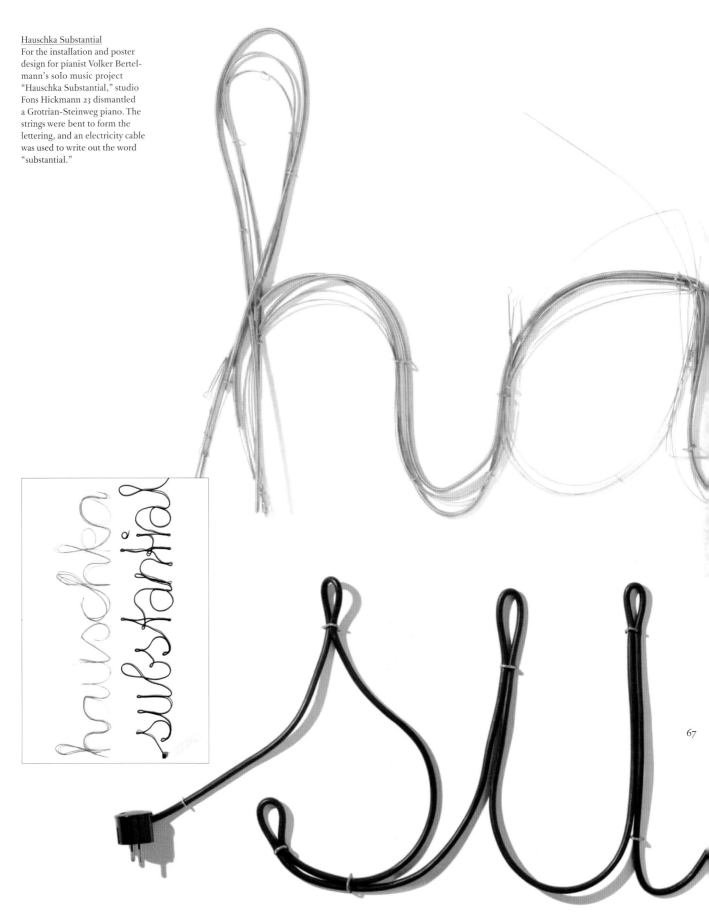

Hauschka Substantial
For the installation and poster design for pianist Volker Bertelmann's solo music project "Hauschka Substantial," studio Fons Hickmann 23 dismantled a Grotrian-Steinweg piano. The strings were bent to form the lettering, and an electricity cable was used to write out the word "substantial."

67

Give
Using nearly two miles of thread
and several hundred steel pins,
Colombian-born, Miami-based
designer Camilo Rojas created
Give for a Macy's holiday window
display. Cleverly designing the
word with the very material
of fashion, Rojas connects the
holiday spirit with the sartorial
gifts showcased inside. The project
exhibits his general commitment
to playfulness as a productive
approach to typographic design.

Question & Answer on page 218

CAMILO ROJAS

Using just a roll of pink vinyl
and some tent stakes, University
of Brighton student Katie Davies
devised a typographic system for
the music label r/n. The synthetic
material pops against the mono-
chromatic swath of green, creating
a spledid juxtaposition.

Side A
The Good Earth (3:29)

Side B
Man the Destroyer (4:52)

69

KATIE DAVIES

Chapter 3

71

GYÖNGY LAKY

GO And..., Estuary,
Domain Change and Negative
(Clockwise from top left)
San Francisco-based artist Gyöngy
Laky creates sculptural, site-specific,
typographic work composed primarily
of debris from orchards and municipal
pruning, and occasionally, wire, nails,
screws, commercial lumber, and
post-consumer waste. Citing "human
ingenuity" as an inspiration, Laky
is intrigued by simple, improvisational
structures like scaffolds and fences
and by the development of letters,
numbers, and symbols, which "construct linear elements into something
useful and clever." The ampersand,
whose form is taken from a ligatured
"et" (Latin for "and"), is an example
of this. But Laky also likes the ampersand's form for its nonessential
meaning: "My association with the
ampersand is its linking role and a kind
of optimism that it is able to suggest."

GYÖNGY LAKY

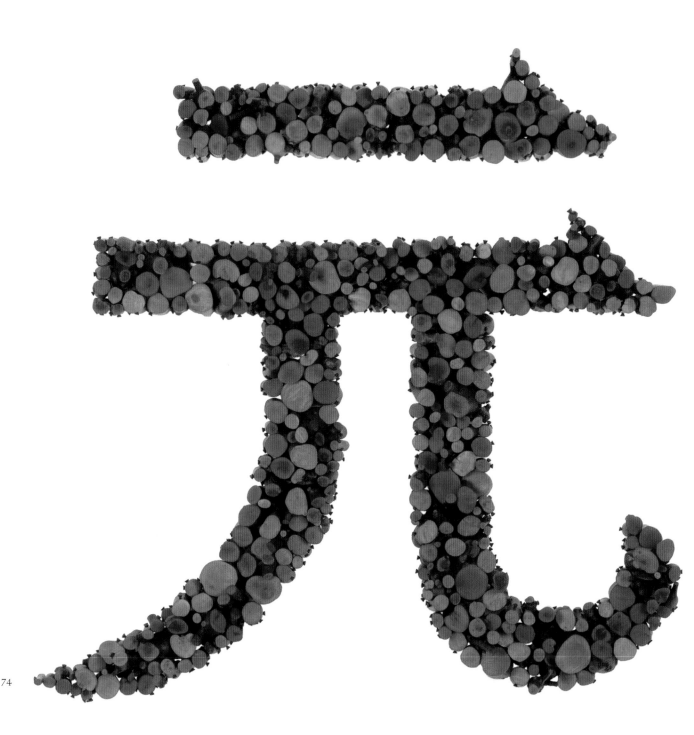

GYÖNGY LAKY

Give and Take and
Longing for Tomorrow
In 2004, Laky was commissioned
to create a work relating to US
currency. "At that time I was actively
producing a series of works that
touched upon my aversion to war
and opposition to the war in Iraq,"
she explains. "I created a charcoal
dollar sign embedded with small,
black, plastic soldiers. I also created
two US cent symbols in 2007,
spurring my interest in monetary
symbols." In 2009, Laky completed
Give and Take (the Chinese Yuan,
left) and Longing For Tomorrow
(the Japanese Yen, right). The series
has coincidently connected Laky's
work to the current global finan-
cial crisis.
Question & Answer on page 216

75

GYÖNGY LAKY

Typographer and graphic designer
Clotilde Olyff has spent the last
20 years combing beaches to collect
and assemble nearly 30 stone
alphabets, which, she asserts, have
not been "re-touched"! Olyff
is a lecturer at the National Visual
Art School of La Cambre and
Art School "75," both in Brussels.
Question & Answer on page 217

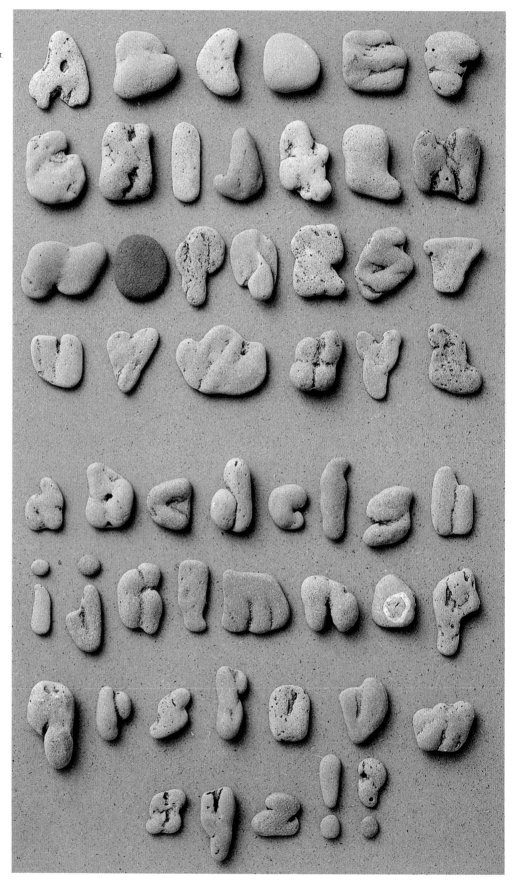

76

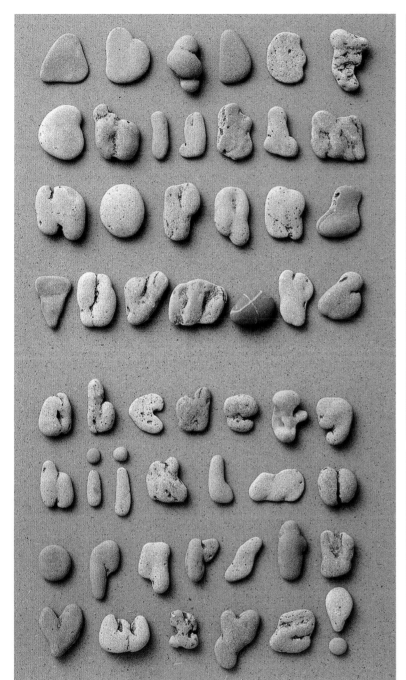
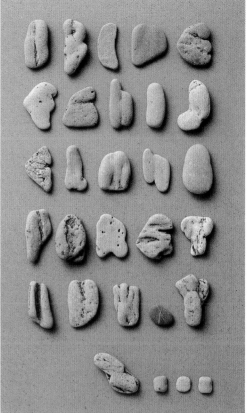

CLOTILDE OLYFF

Shakespeare 1, 2 and 3
Designer and illustrator Anna Garforth's living texts inhabit a space between the natural and artificial world. The designer collaborated with Eleanor Stevens to create large-scale "moss art" pieces for various exhibitions and clients. For The Royal Shakespeare Company in Stratford, the duo was asked to illustrate a quotation from *Much Ado About Nothing*: "There was a star danced, and under that was I born." In addition to living typography, Garforth is also interested in applying other natural and recycled materials to her design work, which ranges from identity and editorial print work to illustration and installation.

Question & Answer on page 215

Prophet (right)
Prophet was exhibited in Perugia, Italy, for the "Over Design Over" exhibition. For this exhibition Garforth and Stevens chose a quotation from Khalil Gibran's *The Prophet*: "If this is my day of harvest, in what fields have I sown my seeds?"

Sporeborne (below)
"Spore borne air represents winds of change, feeling of movement, setting seeds, moisture, potential," says Garforth.

78

ANNA GARFORTH / ELEANOR STEVENS

Autumn

Kyle Bean's interest in "physical type" takes a literal bent with the self-initiated project <u>Autumn</u>. After collecting a variety of fallen leaves and categorizing them by color, he spelled out "autumn" in its associative form. Where there used to be a scattering of random colored leaves on the ground, a direct message stands in its place. A recent graduate of the University of Brighton, Bean has a keen interest in creating typography from gathered objects and hand-crafted models.

Degree Show Announcement
For the University of Brighton's
2009 Degree show, Kyle Bean,
along with collaborators Josh
White and Rory Taylor, created
type out of synthetic fur and pipe
cleaners. The typographic mous-
tache and Victorian costumes
reference the 150th Anniversary
of Brighton Art School.

81

KYLE BEAN

A Origem da Obra de Arte
(The Origin of the Work of Art)
For Marilá Dardot's solo exhibition
"Projeto Pampulha: Marilá Dardot,"
at Museu de Arte da Pampulha
in Brazil, she invited visitors to
the museum to seed letter-shaped
planters. The pots were left to grow
throughout the duration of the
exhibition.

Explorers

For this collaboration with Arts In Area Development, Autobahn made a small but congenial publication, which contained ideas for placing art in developing areas. The cover image is inspired by the series "Landscapes" by photographer Levi van Veluw.

Question & Answer on page 210

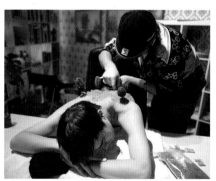

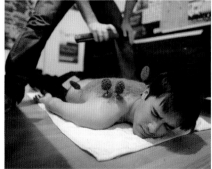

AUTOBAHN

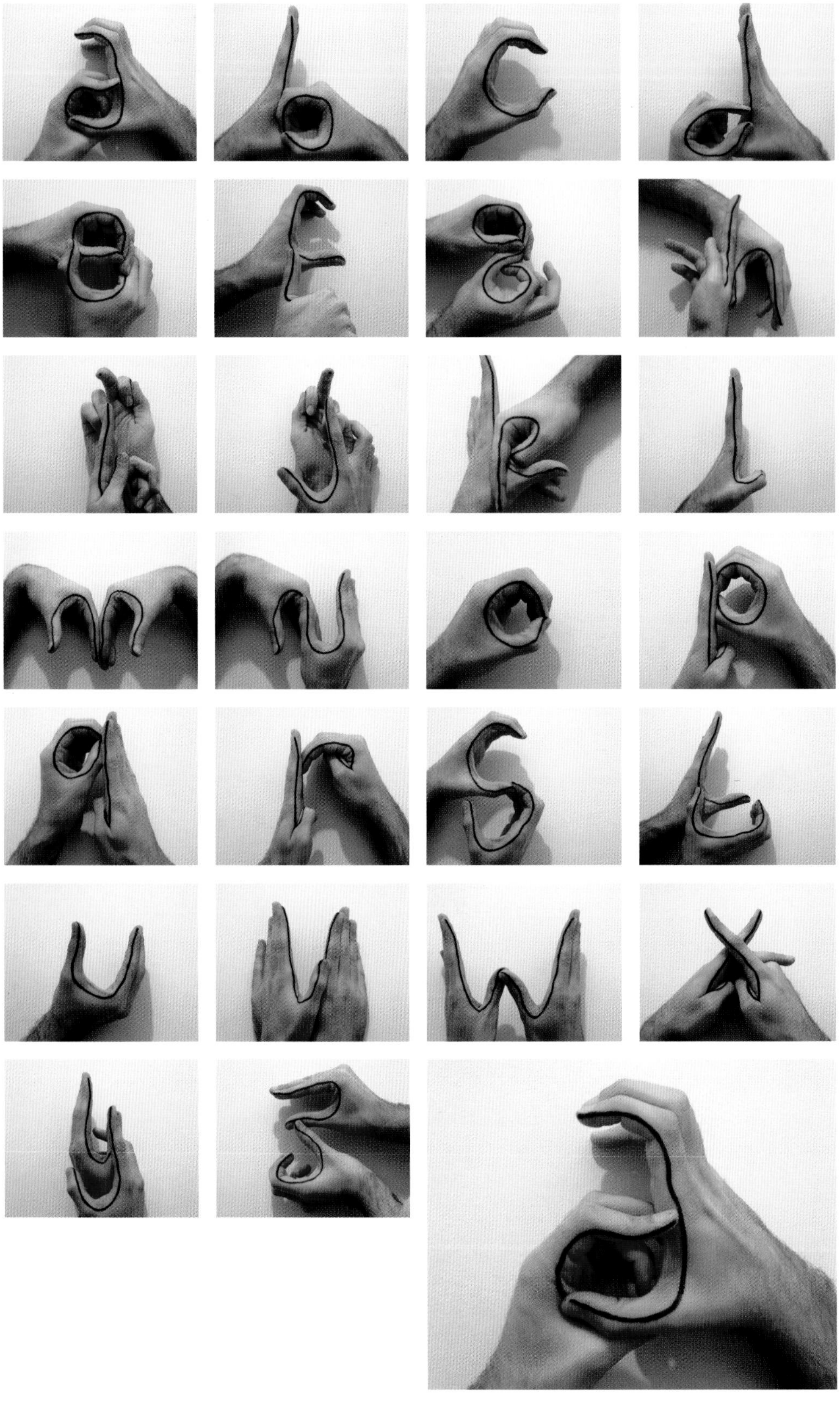

Hand Letters
Paris-based designer Jean de
Trémontels set out to create
a modular, hand-drawn font—
literally with his own two hands.
After trying a variety of approaches, de Trémontels decided to draw
lines along the outside ridge of his
hands. In this way, he was better
able to delineate the letterforms.

84

85

RHETT DASHWOOD

Depression and Emphatica (NO)
Lance Winn created <u>Depression</u>
out of cut, stacked paper by tracing
the word "depression" and then
cutting it out with an Xacto knife.
Each subsequent layer is created
from the mistakes of the last.
The result is a topography generated from the word "depression."
<u>Emphatica (NO)</u> started as a test
for the word "nothing." It is made
by tracing the text with spray-
foam so that each subsequent layer
responds to the previous layer.

86

87

The Hairy Wishes
Now based in Oslo, the French designer 5ive's hirsute typographic experiments play with form and language. In January 2009 5ive created the hairy letters as an attempt at a comical New Year's greeting, playing off the fact that the Norwegian word "hår" (hair) rhymes with "år" (year).

Eyelash Typeface

Iranian-born graphic designer
Amitis Pahlevan created this typeface out of fake eylashes and glue.
The effect is at once diffuse and
arresting, as the pared down letterforms jump—or curl—off the
page. Pahlevan graduted from
the University of California, Long
Beach with a degree in graphic
design; she currently lives and
works in New York City.

For this typeface Stockholm-based animator and designer Björn Johansson took inspiration from the Marshall McLuhan quotation "the medium is the message"— "the idea that it is the media itself, rather than the content it holds, that should be the concern of our study." Using high-contrast lighting, Johansson's hands become less readable, while the letterforms are brought to the fore.

89

BJÖRN JOHANSSON

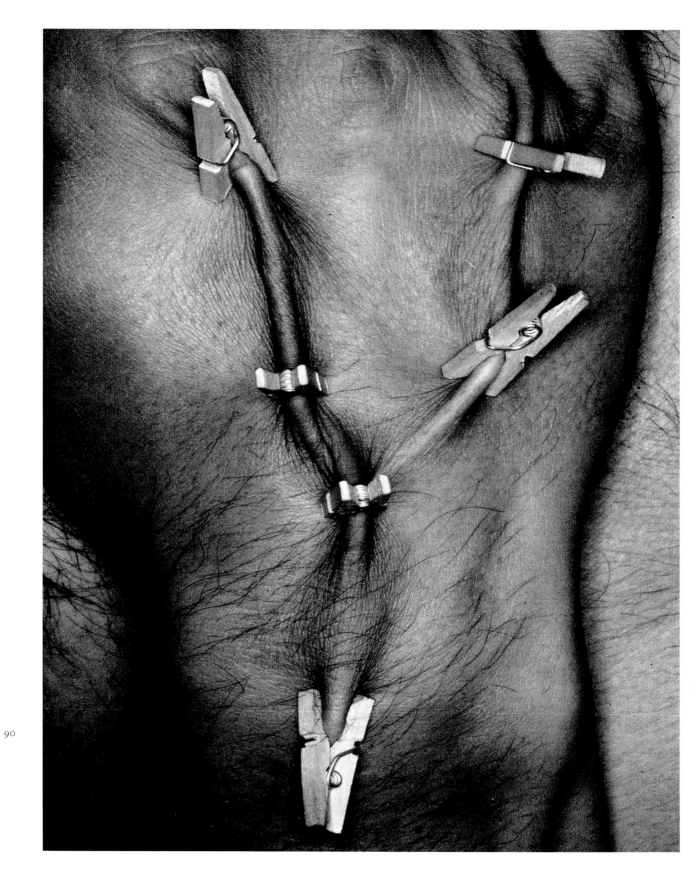

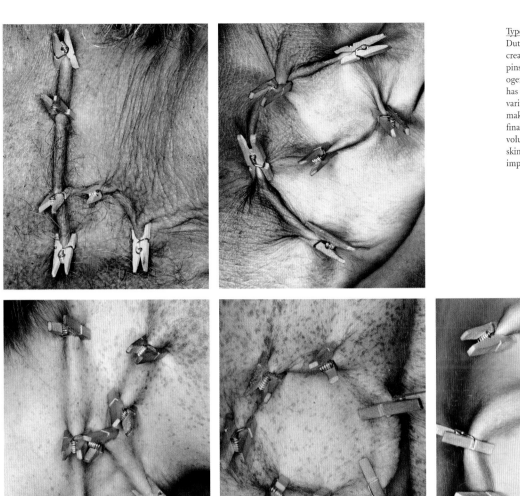

Dutch designer Thijs Verbeek created an alphabet using clothespins and skin to create a heterogeneous character set. Each letter has its own quality due to the variation in skin and body types, making it hard to predict the final shape. Fleshy skin results in voluptuous characters, while taut skin gives the letterforms a narrow, imperfect shape.

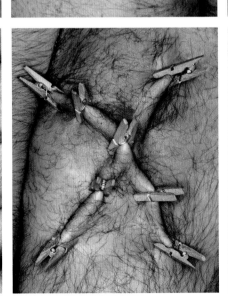

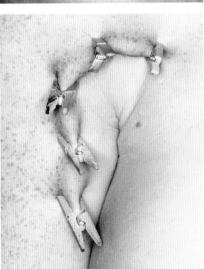

91

THIJS VERBEEK

JOCELYN COTTENCIN

Vocabulario Series

Rennes, France-based designer Jocelyn Cottencin's dance and type experiments <u>Just a Walk</u> and <u>Landscape</u> are part of his "Vocabulario" series of anthropomorphic typefaces. The series is done in collaboration with other artists and designers, and exhibited through a variety of mediums like the ten screen television "settlement" at left.

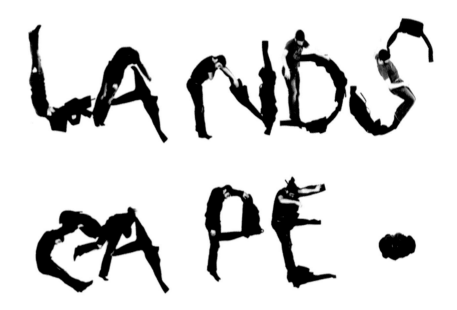

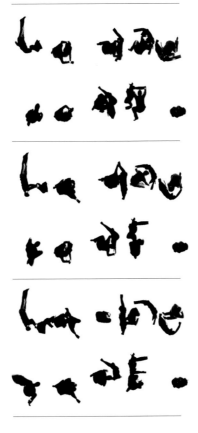

93

JOCELYN COTTENCIN

94

HandMadeFont is tirelessly searching for new material with which to render type. Brothers and founders Vladimir and Maksim Loginov created this quirky lower-case font out of hair.

Nella Mia Città Nessuno è Straniero
(In My Town Nobody is a Stranger)
Verona, Italy-based designers
Happycentro created this non-
profit campaign to promote
cultural integration. Through in-
formal and academic workshops
the designers created giant letterforms—with participants photographed alongside them—to
spell out Nella Mia Città Nessuno
è Straniero.

Amandine Alessandra is a French graphic designer based in London. Her work often plays with language and double meaning. Obscene, for example, explores contextual lettering—how to render a letter so that it can be read in two ways. Legttering plays off of the anatomical references in typographic vocabulary—anatomy, body size, head piece, footers, etc. The same goes for a book's design with its head, joints, spine, back, and foot.

98

99

AMANDINE ALESSANDRA

Chapter

1
2
3
4
5
6

STEFAN SAGMEISTER
AMANDINE ALESSANDRA
HIKARU FURUHASHI
ANNA GARFORTH /
   ELEANOR STEVENS
OWEN GILDERSLEEVE
CLAIRE MORGAN
BELA BORSODI
MIGUEL RAMIREZ
HANDMADEFONT
CLOTILDE OLYFF
ANDREW BYROM
TYPEWORKSHOP
ED NACIONAL
SVETLANA SEBYAKINA
MILES GOULD /
   JOE LUXTON
KATIES DAVIES
D. BILLY
THOMAS VOORN
CHANGBAE SEO /
   ETHAN PARK
JAMIE THOMPSON
DAN TOBIN SMITH
CC'S
ASA~AMA
GANZ TOLL
KEETRA DEAN DIXON
LEE STOKES
ODED EZER
BAGS OF JOY
JONATHAN ZAWADA
LABOUR
CAMILO ROJAS
BANK™
AUTOBAHN

"I rarely obsess about things in
my private life," explains Stefan
Sagmeister. "However, I do obsess
over our work and think that
a number of [Sagmeister Inc.'s]
better projects came out of such
an obsession." In an installation
of 250,000 Eurocents on Waag-
dragerhof Square in Amsterdam,
Sagmeister—along with the help
of more than 100 volunteers over
8 days—wrote out "Obsessions
make my life worse and my work
better." After completion the coins
were left free and unguarded for
the public to interact with. Less
than 20 hours after the grand
opening, a local resident noticed
a person bagging the coins and
taking them away. Protective of
the design piece they had watched
being created, they called the
police. After stopping the "crimi-
nal" the police—in an effort to
"preserve" the artwork—swept up
every remaining cent and carted
it all away.

103

STEFAN SAGMEISTER

Having / Guts / Always /
Works Out / For / Me.
For a 2003 issue of the Austrian
magazine *Copy*, Sagmeister
designed six spreads, spaced intermittently throughout the book,
which read: "Having / guts / always /
works out / for / me." Each
photographic piece introduces
a new section of the magazine.
Question & Answer on page 219

STEFAN SAGMEISTER

AMANDINE ALESSANDRA

Booksetting

UK-based designer Amandine Alessandra's series is based on Thomas Fuller's statement "a book that is shut is but a block." Alessandra used shut books as building blocks. Shelves are used as a typographic grid, and the books are considered merely for their shape and color, rather than content. Alessandra's arrangement recalled typesetting processes, as every type made of colored books had to be blocked with white books, just as it is done in letterpress, where large areas of white space are created by wooden blocks called "furniture."

AMANDINE ALESSANDRA

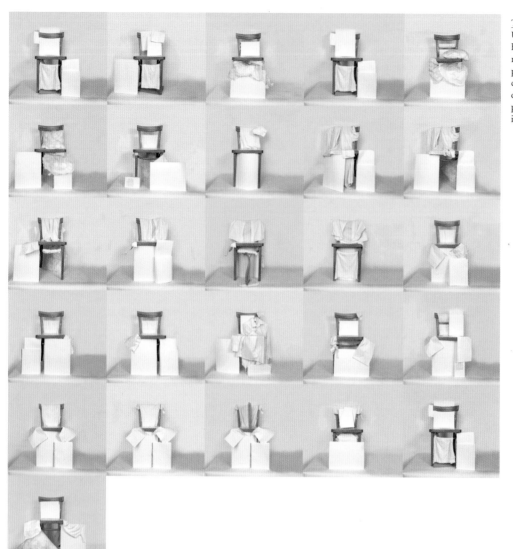

Take a Seat and Say Something
Using a white pillow, white note-book, and white shirt, Alessandra reveals letterforms by obscuring portions of a chair. Though the characters are some what inde-cipherable on their own, when presented in a group they become instantly distinguishable.

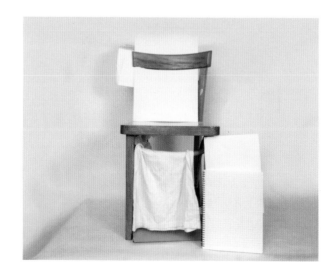

<u>Cafe de Chill and
Open Frameworks</u>
Wonder Wonder is a New York
City-based multidisciplinary
creative studio founded by Hikaru
Furuhashi. The studio practices
and exhibits graphic works with a
focus on the conceptual, the playful, and the handmade. <u>Cafe de
Chill</u>—a poster concept for an
electronic-folk music event in
Tokyo (top)—uses hand-assembled
found objects for a software company called Open Frame.

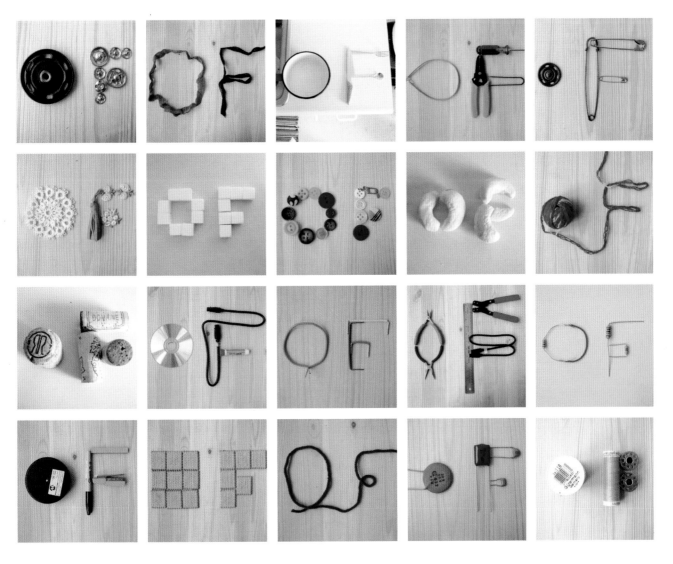

HIKARU FURUHASHI

ANNA GARFORTH / ELEANOR STEVENS

Anna Garforth and Eleanor Stevens
taught a workshop called Trash
Type at London College of
Communication. The project
brief was to create a word communicating its medium. The students
collected a week's worth of trash,
after which each individual piece
was rolled into a tight tube and
assembled to form the word "used."
Question & Answer on page 215

ANNA GARFORTH / ELEANOR STEVENS

For issue 12 of *Graphic* magazine,
UK-based Owen Gildersleeve
created type out of outmoded
cassettes and records for an article
about the customization of different musical formats. September
was a typographic illustration
comissioned by *Fast Company*
magazine to be used in their
front-of-book calendar section.

113

OWEN GILDERSLEEVE

Perch (Crowdpleaser) and Animal Magnetism

London-based artist Claire Morgan has exhibited internationally, with solo shows, residencies, and commissions across the UK, as well as group exhibitions in Europe. At an early stage she developed a strong interest in the organic, in natural processes, and in the bodily connotations of natural materials. This formed the basis for her sculptural installations and continues to influence her work at present.

Perch was the culmination of a residency at Persistence Works Studios, Sheffield, UK, in 2006 (below). For the exhibition, thousands of fragments of torn white polythene were suspended on horizontal threads, spelling out the word "crowdpleaser." A decaying crow was perched on the letter "a." For Animal Magnetism (opposite page) Morgan designed a barrier, which was composed of nylon threads stretched horizontally, with fragments of torn pink polythene recycling bags threaded through each.

CLAIRE MORGAN

BELA BORSODI

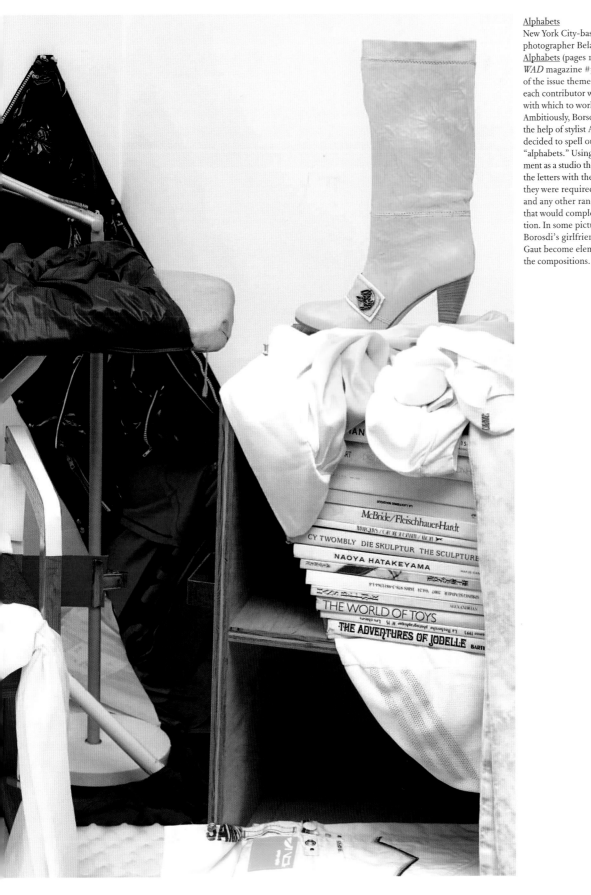

Alphabets

New York City-based, Austrian photographer Bela Borsodi shot Alphabets (pages 116–121) for *WAD* magazine #39. In light of the issue theme "Alphabets," each contributor was given a letter with which to work; his was "A." Ambitiously, Borsodi (along with the help of stylist Akari Endo-Gaut) decided to spell out the word "alphabets." Using Borsodi's apartment as a studio the pair constructed the letters with the fashion items they were required to photograph and any other random object that would complete the composition. In some pictures Bordosi, Borosdi's girlfriend, and Endo-Gaut become elements within the compositions.

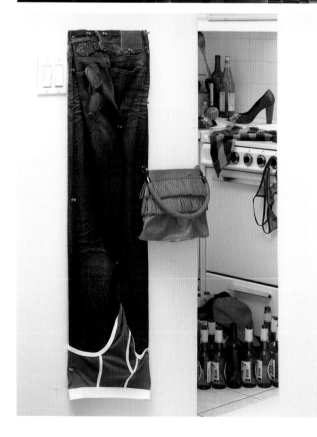

BELA BORSODI

119

BELA BORSODI

BELA BORSODI

BELA BORSODI

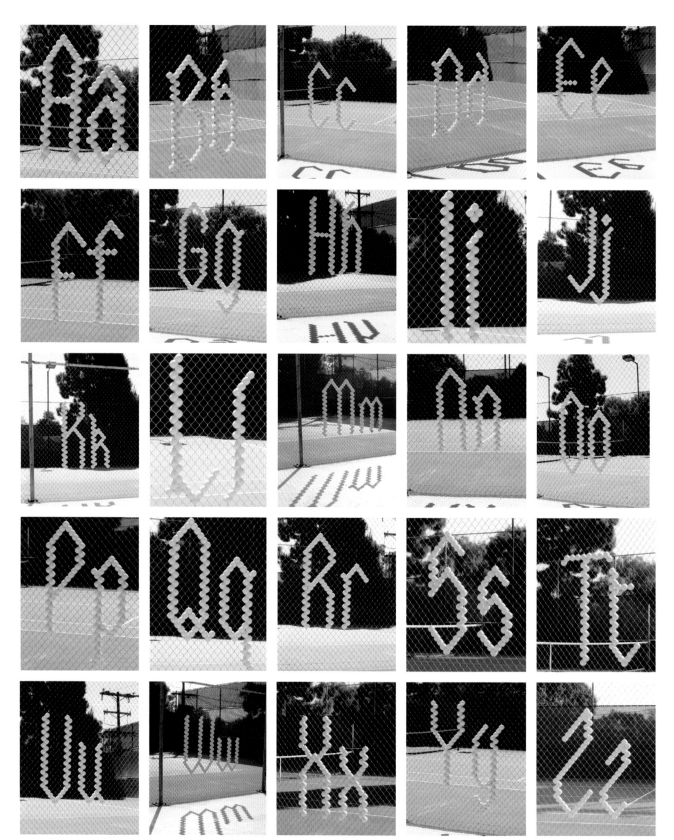

MIGUEL RAMIREZ

Beeep Beep Beeeeep and Love
Los Angeles-based graphic
designer Miguel Ramirez created
two conceptual typefaces out of
familiar objects. For Love, in
collaboration with Melissa Madrid,
tennis balls create a dot matrix
font. For Beeep Beep Beeeeep he
used grocery store paper bags
to create 3D type.

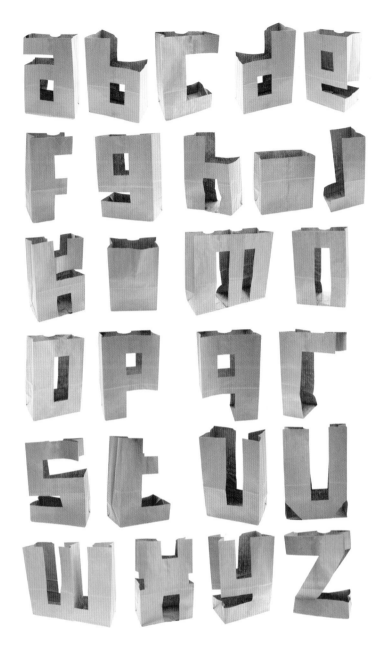

MIGUEL RAMIREZ

Bap
HandMadeFont designers
(and brothers) Vladimir and
Maksim Loginov designed
humorous typefaces using
grandmother's dough recipe
and an oven.

124

Sandwich Alphabet

Belgain graphic designer and typographer Clotilde Olyff created this sandwich alphabet from real dried bread, however, the salad, eggs, and tomatoes are inedibly made of painted paper. Olyff's work is varied and ranges from typography and identity work to stamps, packaging, and poster design.

Question & Answer on page 217

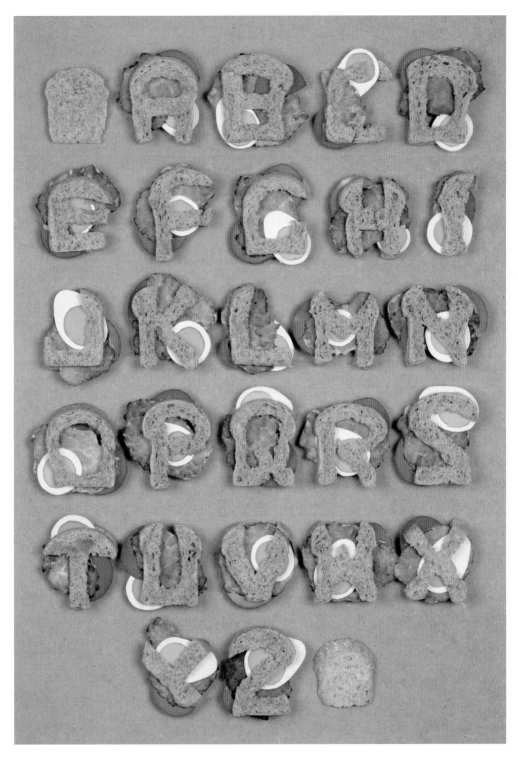

CLOTILDE OLYFF

Grab-Me

Andrew Byrom's Grab-Me is constructed out of bathroom handrails (or grab-bars) and its design adheres, almost perfectly, to the breaks found in typographic stencil designs. Completed in 2006, it is a full alphabet set made from 1.5-inch diameter stainless steel tubing with a 180 grit brushed finish. These finished typographic handrails are intended for use in swimming pools or bathrooms. They can be used indoors, or as building signage.

Venetian

In 2008 Byrom was commissioned to design a stencil typeface by *Elle Decoration* (UK magazine); Venetian is inspired by the forms created when opening and closing a venetian blind.

Question & Answer on page 211

ANDREW BYROM

ANDREW BYROM

Say Goodbye for the Digital Pixels
—Be Natural, Be a True Craftsman!
In a typography workshop by
Underware at Ecole Cantonale
d'Art de Lausanne, Switzerland,
students designed manually
pixelated letters. After choosing
a repeatable shape, like an open
book or a grocery cart, the creation
of the letterforms became intuitive;
judging the letterforms by eye
became a much more valuable skill
than using a geometric grid.
Question & Answer on page 221

129

Tiepography

Ed Nacional, a Brooklyn-based Canadian designer, created a display typeface constructed from his personal tie collection. "A large amount of the collection was acquired from my dad," he explains. "The rest I bought at flea markets and thrift stores with a few brand new purchases sprinkled throughout. I hope to soon extend this project to add alternates, numbers, and ligatures as the collection grows."

130

8:00 | Good Morning
For this series Moscow-based graphic designer Svetlana Sebyakina creates a new typographic work each morning. Sebyakina uses both handmade and found objects to create her pieces. For these installments, the designer used corn and slinkies to greet the day. (Project continues on page 53.)

132

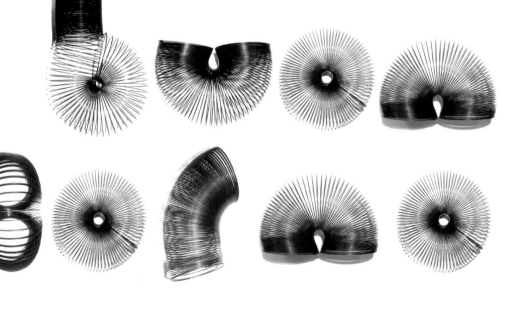

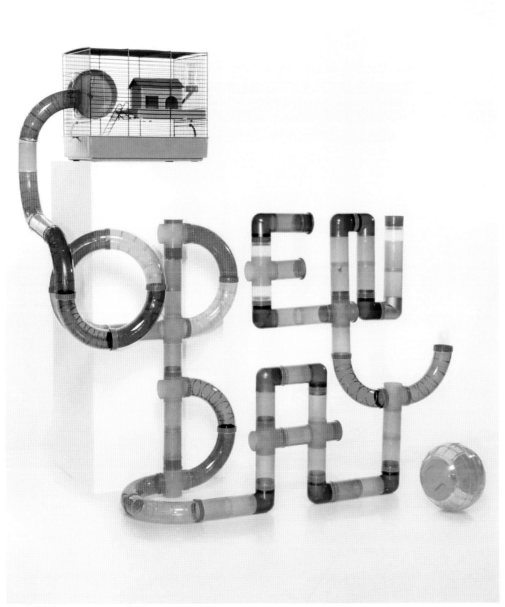

UK-based desigers Miles Gould
and Joe Luxton's winning poster
and leaflet design for Brighton
University Open Days uses a wide
variety of colored plastic Rotastack
hamster tubing, tunnels, and
extension units to create type.
The poster suggests the idea of
an institution (the hamster cage)
with the Rotastack offering an
alternative, colorful, and stimulat-
ing experience outside the box.
The pair collaborated with Claude
d'Avoine on the project.

133

MILES GOULD / JOE LUXTON

UK-based designer Katie Davies
designed a poster pitch (collaborating with Maiko Yamazaki)
for Brighton University Open Days
publicity campaign, using balloons
and a bucket of water.

134

Fooosh, Rrring, and Crackle

Brooklyn-based designer David William (D.Billy) created a number of site interventions, using colorful media such as twisting balloons, party streamers, and artist tape to add visual representations of sound effects in public spaces. For William, these projects encourage a reexamination of surroundings and objects that are usually taken for granted, and "hopefully inject a hint of fantastical surreality into the lives of anyone who happens upon them."

135

D.BILLY

THOMAS VOORN

Garment Graffiti

Dutch designer and art director
Thomas Voorn creates tension
between text and the physical
environment by using clothes to
create Garment Graffiti in the most
obvious and unexpected places,
from brick walls and alleys to
sun-kissed fields. Projects like
"The Clothing Alphabet" in 2006
and "The Fashion Hit Next Season"
series create a "colorful landscape
pollution" that is environmentally
friendly.

THOMAS VOORN

The work of Chang Bae Seo and Ethan Park combines their interest in fashion and graphic design. For the project, they constructed type from colorful garments hung over a banner, socks tacked to the wall, and shoes arranged on the ground to form the message "Function Follows Form." The arrangement mirrors the hierarchy of everyday dress.

138

Freak

Jamie Thompson designed cover art for the Yo Majesty Halloween single release in collaboration with Abi Green and Rex McWhirter. The team produced a series of record covers responding to the track title "Freak." This cover featured a professionally formed balloon dog, which, due to its perfection, seemed freakish. The reverse side featured an amateur balloon dog made from the same balloon.

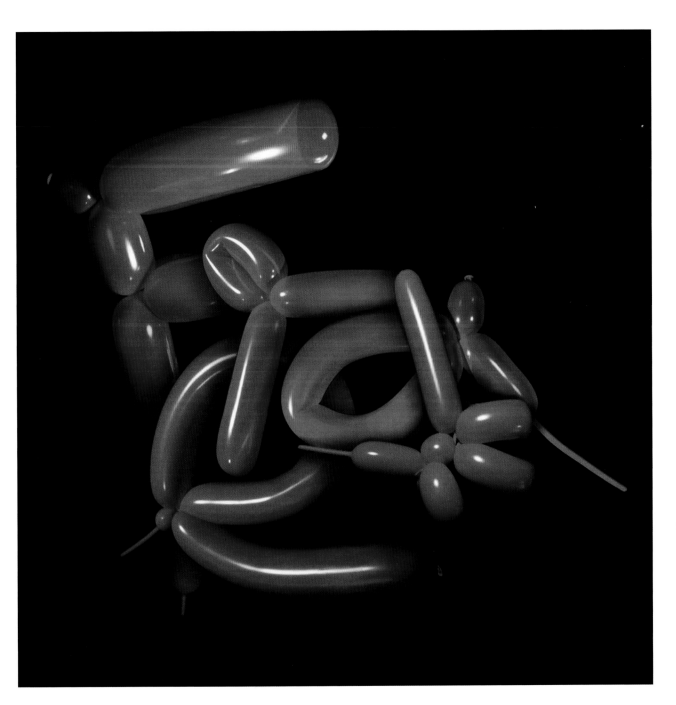

139

DAN TOBIN SMITH

E, T, and A

A London native, Dan Tobin Smith composes and photographs highly inventive assemblages for major commercial clients. *The Creative Review* commissioned Smith to compose the <u>A</u> out of photography equipment, taking into account the perspective of studio space.

Subsequently, Smith was hired to create a similar project for *The New York Times's T* magazine. For a personal project, the photographer composed a dichromatic <u>E</u> out of red and white ephemera, manipulating perspective to form a sans serif letterform. Smith graduated from Central St. Martin's with a degree in art and design and received his Master's in photography from London College of Printing. <u>Question & Answer on page 220</u>

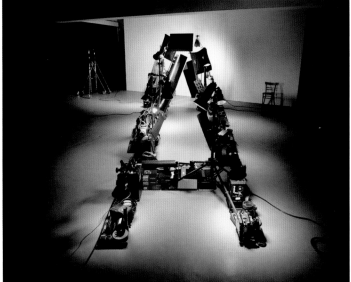

DAN TOBIN SMITH

Y, B, A, and E

New York City-based photographers, CC's, collaborated on Christmas cards, using simple, organic 3D type. They were so pleased with the results, that the pair began photographing the alphabet in the same way.

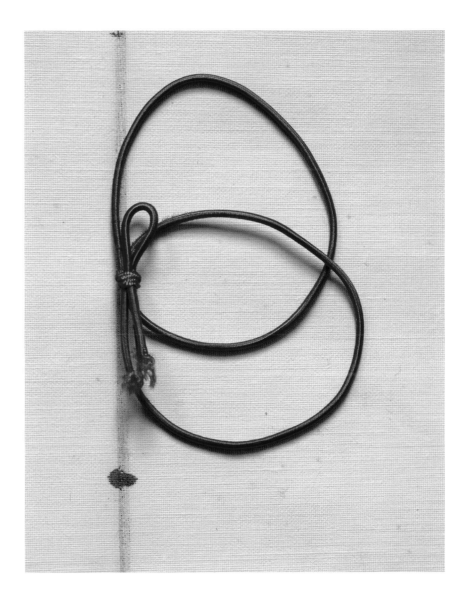

CC'S

The Torino, Italy-based design studio asa~ama created these frail, metal letterforms covered with recycled elements. The typface is inspired by the folk art movement, primitivism, and the occult.

Flash Mob!
Every year in Buenos Aires,
a pillowfight called Flash Mob!
takes place. Pablo Colabella
and Santiago Fernández of the
Argentinean design firm Ganz
Toll designed the event poster
in which the type was made
of real feathers.

145

As Long as I Can
New York City-based artist and designer Keetra Dean Dixon's (FromKeetra) socially themed projects are notorious for their friendly absurdism and whimsical tone. In this example, the word "until," is constructed out of sand timers. The type plays with language by manipulating readability when time is up.

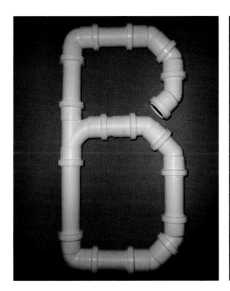

Pipe Font
The modular PVC pipes found at the local hardware store created a surprisingly unified system for London graphic designer Lee Stokes to design the word "flood." The resulting poster embodied a positive message for communities in Britain that were victims of flooding. Stokes's use of standard materials like fittings, valves, bends, and flows makes for an idiosyncratic and subtle typographic composition.

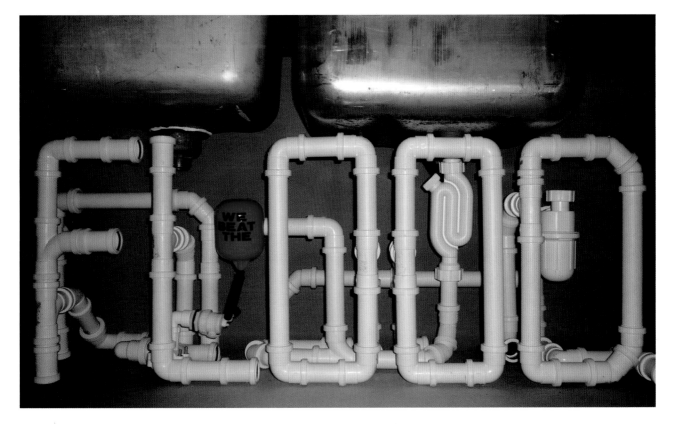

LEE STOKES

Israeli typographic artist and type
designer Oded Ezer designed a
typographic homage to the Israeli
poet Yona Volach, made from
chewing gum (below). The poster
is a response to the poem "Unimportant & Nothing," with the idea
that using a material meant to be
chewed but not consumed suggests
something that is nonessential and
unimportant.

ODED EZER

3D TYPOGRAPHY

Plastica

Ezer created plasticine 3D Hebrew letters that stand on their own feet. The type specimens accompanied *The Plastica Manifesto* written in 2000, which stated: "Contemporary Hebrew type design is being influenced by two sources: By the traditional Hebrew letterforms throughout the history, and by Latin typefaces. Why not add more sources of inspiration? Using the principles of other fields (e.g. biology, architecture, psychology, etc.) in the typographic design will produce new, outstanding creations, in this discipline."

Question & Answer on page 214

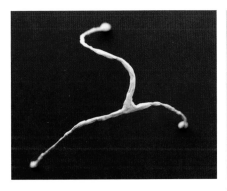

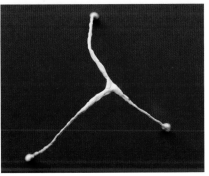

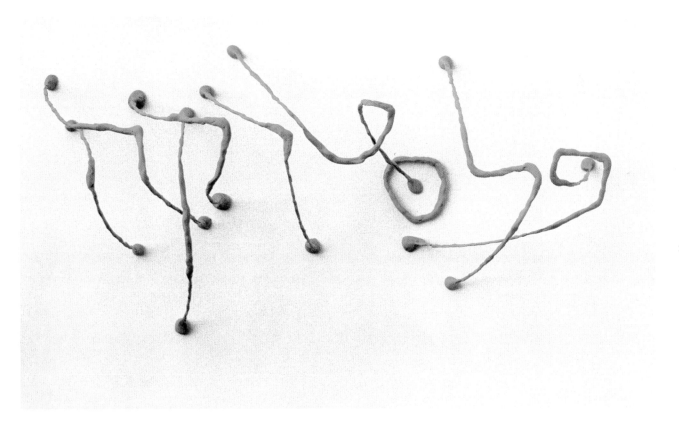

149

ODED EZER

The London-based design collective Bags of Joy—Patrick Cusack, Nick Shea, and George Simkin—geometrically arranged standard wooden clothespins to form type.

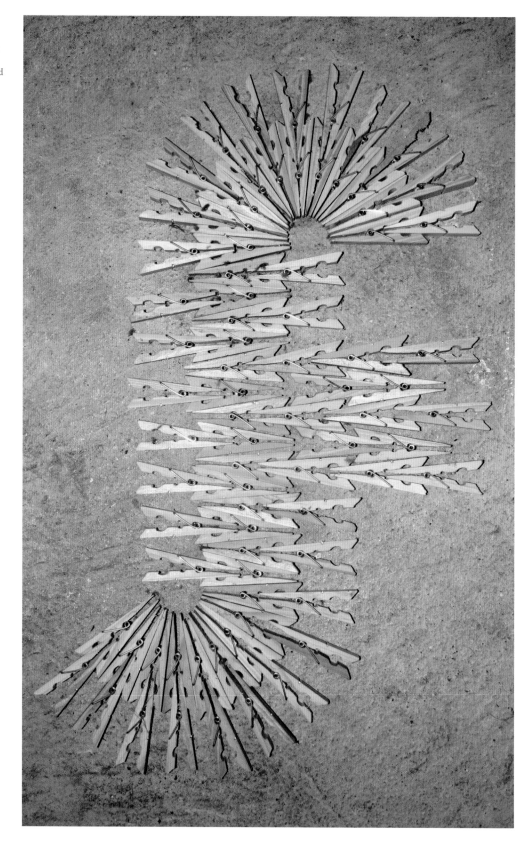

<u>Heart Made of Glass</u>
Australian designer Jonathan Zawada works for various music, art, and fashion clients, employing a diverse range of mediums from website design to illustration. For the band Softlightes's *Heart Made of Glass,* Zawada art directed the music video, which illustrates the song's lyrics using stop-start animation and found objects like silverware, rubber gloves, sugar cubes, and floppy disks, among other things.

151

JONATHAN ZAWADA

THE LOVING SOUNDS OF STATIC
(daytrotter)

Mobius Band Digital Single Cover
For a contribution to the Barack
Rock online music project, in
which contributing musicians were
paired with visual artists, Brooklyn-
based design firm Labour created a
track image for Mobius Band. The
designers hung found objects with
monofilament and wire inside
an old silkscreen frame and photographed the final composition.

152

AIGA Move Conference Poster
For the AIGA New York chapter, Labour was asked to design a graphics package for a conference focusing on motion, film, and design. The concept included everything from posters to pamphlets, video, tote bags, and signage. For the packaging, the designers constructed a unit-based typeface from wooden blocks and photographed it against different backgrounds, using stop-motion animation to bring the composition to life.

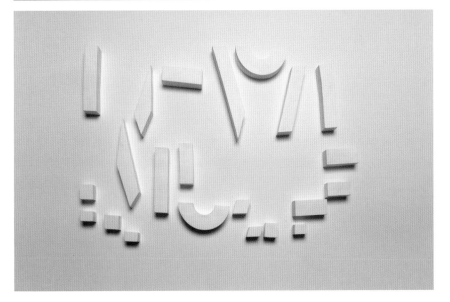

153

154

Enjoy, Flavor and Gold (Consumption)

This series's intention is to expose the deceitful nature of advertising by turning companies' messages into the opposite of their marketing objective. Gold criticizes a popular fast food company and its contribution to the obesity problem facing our society today. Graphic designer Camilo Rojas, created the piece using golden french fries to spell out the word "gold." Similarly, Enjoy—a piece composed of over 18,000 soda-rusted nails driven into a wood canvas—and the 3,000 cigarette Flavor, criticize the soft drink and cigarette industries for marketing products that are detrimental to people's health.

Question & Answer on page 218

155

CAMILO ROJAS

<u>Pneuma</u>
Berlin-based Sebastian Bissinger
and Laure Boer—French and
German, respectively—have run
the design studio BANK™ since
2007. For the typeface they used
a flat tire to create all the letters
in the alphabet; the work was
incidentally inspired by Boer's
tendency to pop bicycle tires.

156

Arts the Beatdoctor
Autobahn designed typographic, band-aid band shirts for hip-hop artist Bas Vermolen (aka Art the Beatdoctor) to be sold at venues and online shops. Vermolen's debut album *Transitions* was released by Unexpected Records in 2007. On the album, Art collaborated with Pete Philly, Skiggy Rapz and The Proov.

Question & Answer on page 210

157

Chapter

ANDREW BYROM
DEAN KAUFMAN
JANNO HAHN
RICHARD J. EVANS
KARSTEN SCHMIDT
STUDIO NEWWORK /
    REONA UEDA
FRANK TJEPKEMA
STEPHANIE DEARMOND
DAVID ASPINALL
MULTISTOREY
JULIEN DE REPENTIGNY
KEETRA DEAN DIXON /
    JK KELLER
MIKE PERRY /
    JAY BELL
STEFAN SAGMEISTER
TYPEWORKSHOP
NICK VAN WOERT
HUDA ABDUL AZIZ
LISA RIENERMANN
JOHN BECKERS
MARILA DARDOT
THORBJØRN ANKERSTJERNE
AUTOBAHN
ERIC KU
KERSTIN LANDIS /
    NAIMA SCHALCHER /
    MARTINA WALTHERT
TOBIAS BATTENBERG
OSCAR & EWAN
JAMES GRIFFIN
JÓNAS VALTÝSSON
BIWA
ALIDA ROSIE SAYER
G&V
JOHN CASERTA
JAS BHACHU
HUMANS SINCE 1982
CHARLES MAZÉ
MIGUEL RAMIREZ
DAVID MARSH
CHRISTIAAN POSTMA
ALVIN ARONSON
DATENSTRUDEL /
    MARK FORMANEK

159

Los Angeles-based designer and typographer Andrew Byrom is interested in the ways in which the limitations of new materials and processes help to inform—or force—the outcome of a design. Once an initial concept is devised, Byrom selects a material that will further dictate its execution. For Byrom, working with 3D letterforms allows him to move out of his "comfort-zone" and design from a new standpoint. His work takes into consideration typographic principles (uniformed x-height, structure, etc.) as well as architectural integrity. These explorations have led him to unexpected design arenas like furniture and package design.

Letter-Box-Kite
Byrom's experimental series of 26 typographic kites is fabricated from thin nylon fabric and fiberglass poles.

TSS2

This proposal for a low-cost temporary signage system is fabricated from corrugated plastic with peel-off segments, revealing a white background that enables every letter (upper and lower cases) and number to be constructed. The design, which is lightweight and flat-packed, is intended for indoor or outdoor use in shops, cafes, conferences, gallery openings, etc.

St. Louis

This modular design was commissioned by ASIFA-Hollywood, the Los Angeles chapter of the International Animated Film Society. The logo and typeface were designed to work for print, digital animation, and 3D fabrication for award trophies. An on-screen animated version of the logo was produced in collaboration with Hollywood animator Aubry Mintz (Industrial Light and Magic/Square).

ANDREW BYROM

This temporary "pop-up" sign-age system is fabricated from water-proof nylon wrapped around a fiberglass pole frame (similar to the construction of a modern dome tent). An elastic cord running inside the hollow poles allows the design to collapse into a small bag for storage. The design is intended for use in shops, galleries, conferences, etc.

162

Interiors Light

This initial concept was inspired by Marcel Breuer's Wassily Chair and was intended to be a rounded chrome tubular steel version like the iconic chair design and based off the letterforms of <u>Interiors</u>. As the project developed, Byrom realized that by working at a smaller scale, each letter could be constructed in neon. The limitations of working in neon were difficult, and the design had to be re-worked several times to embrace the constraints of this beautiful and delicate material.

Interiors

Originally conceived as a digital font, <u>Interiors</u> (right) was inspired by an old wooden chair in the corner of Byrom's London office that, when looked at from a certain angle, resembled the letter "h." Using the 3D principles of this simple form, and closely adhering to type design conventions, the 26 letters of the alphabet were drawn and generated as a font. They were later constructed in 3D form, using tubular steel to create full-scale furniture frames. Because the underlying design concept is typographical, the end result becomes almost freestyle furniture design. Letters like "m," "n," "o," "b," and "h" can be viewed as simple tables and chairs, but other letters, like "e," "g," "a," "s," "t," "v," "x," and "z" become beautiful abstract pieces of furniture.

<u>Question & Answer on page 211</u>

ANDREW BYROM

New York City-based photographer Dean Kaufman was commissioned by art director Jason Miller of Addison Design New York to construct a type-based photo installation for a book project Miller conceived and produced. Kaufman was assigned the word "leaner" and was instructed to use paper tape as the type material. Due to the camera's one-point perspective, the stroke widths and letter heights needed to increase proportionally as they receded into the frame. Type that bled over rafters and onto floors would also need to be accounted for. Employing trigonometry, lasers, and the hands of several collaborators, the text was mapped and built in 11 hours. The manipulative eye of the camera lived up to its potential by representing the 3D contorted and multi-angled tape application as straightforward letterform on the 2D page.

Das Kapital: A Classless Character
Dutch designer Janno Hahn designed the capital "K" by using each letter in the alphabet. Playing off of a basic tenet of communism—that everyone is equal and that each must fill his or her distinct role in a society—he devised an idealogical letterform. "In a classless society all letters are equal," says Hahn, "to build the Kapital K you need to use all 25 of his best friends. It's up to them to stay in balance and not to collapse." The 25 letters are made of 228 pieces of triplex wood.

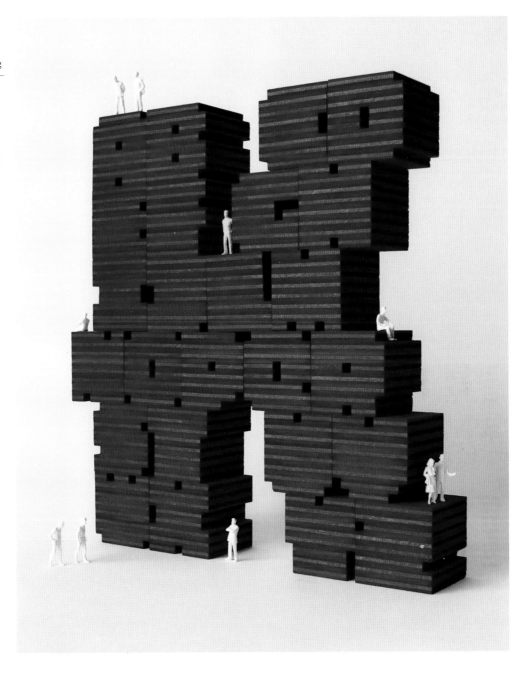

JANNO HAHN

UK-based designer Richard J. Evans's laser-cut wooden letters aim to visually represent the way information is so quickly and easily disseminated through the internet and television. The surfeit of information is at times hard to comprehend and digest, which is why Evans's type is difficult to read.

166

Type & Form

Designer and artist Karsten Schmidt of PostSpectacular designed this typographic sculpture for a cover of *Print* with Kristina Di Matteo and Lindsay Ballant. The piece was designed/grown virtually, using a generative design process based on the manipulated simulation of a biochemical reaction. Using a technique commonly used in medical MRI scan applications, the 2D frames of the various simulation stages were combined into a highly detailed 3D volumetric model, consisting of several million polygons. The piece was printed by Anatol Just (ThingLab), using digital fabrication and the grainy, bone-like printing material reiterates the synthetic biological aesthetic of a seemingly natural, crystalline form. The New York City-based Schmidt is well known for his merging of code writing, design, art, and craft.

167

KARSTEN SCHMIDT

New York City-based Studio Newwork teamed up with Japanese
artist Reona Ueda to create a wear-
able piece of art inspired by *kan-
zashi*, the traditional Japanese hair
ornament. Composed of spiraling
text defining "peace," it is enriched
with handmade representations of
Japanese native plants. The limited
edition pieces are created with
urethane-coated, lacquered synthetic resin, and stainless steel.

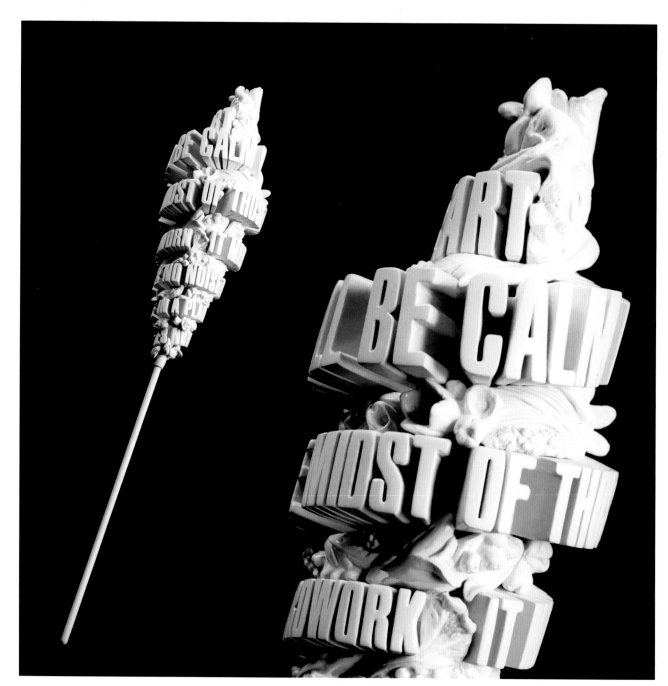

STUDIO NEWWORK / REONA UEDA

3D TYPOGRAPHY

Signature Vases

Dutch designer Frank Tjepkema of Droog created signature vases that literally take their form from the signature of the buyer. Tjepkema scans a signature by means of stereo lithography and from it the form of a distinctly singular vase takes shape. Sadly Droog no longer has the vases in production.

FRANK TJEPKEMA

STEPHANIE DEARMOND

Best/Beast, Dutch Diphthongs
AA, Shy Take, Dutch Diphthongs
(Group), and Hustle 'Em
(Clockwise from top left)
Stephanie DeArmond's work
explores language—taking slang
phrases, colloquialisms, and
snippets of conversation and
abstracting them into sculptural
form where meanings are revealed
and obscured through typography
and letterforms. She uses traditional hand-building techniques
to make complex constructions
from slabs of clay. The typographic
forms she creates are based on
her own hand-drawn lettering.
Each piece is unique—finished
with glazes, vintage ceramic
decals, or painted-on black slip.
Question & Answer on page 213

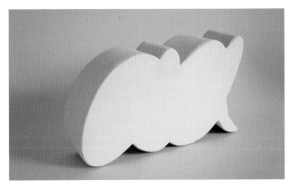

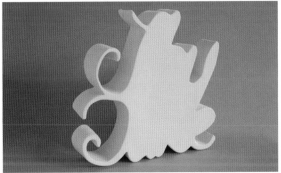

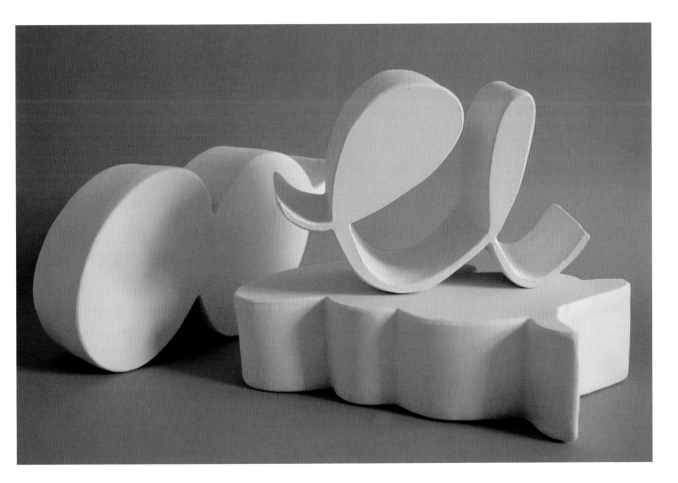

171

STEPHANIE DEARMOND

Magic Type

London-based designer David Aspinall created this short, stop-frame animation—shot over the course of 24 hours—of a "growing" typeface. Using blotting paper, silicone solution, dyes, wood, and glue, Aspinall's letterforms experienced a gradual morphology. The dyed blotting paper characters absorb the silicon solution, causing a chemical reaction, creating vibrant colored crystals.

DAVID ASPINALL

For the Super Design Market
Royal Festival Hall 2007 in
London, Multistorey wrapped
hundreds of meters of fabric
around the structural columns
throughout the large venue;
the studio also created oversize
type made from colored foam.

173

Money, Success, Fame, Glamour
Montreal-based designer Julien
De Repentigny worked with a
quotation from the movie *The
Party Monster* to create type illus-
trations and set designs using
glass and candy.

174

For these two projects designers Keetra Dean Dixon and JK Keller painstakingly created typographic sculptures by layering wax.

KEETRA DEAN DIXON / JK KELLER

A,E,I,O, and U

Graphic designer and illustrator Mike Perry and carpenter and architectural designer Jay Bell collaborated to make these letter-forms. First, Bell constructed the handmade, wooden letterforms, and then Perry embellished them with a paint marker. "I was so amazed at the quality of each character," says Perry, "I didn't want to alter them." Both artists live and work in New York City.

176

Keeping a Diary
Stefan Sagmeister, one of the pioneers of experimental and 3D typography, was invited to Singapore to produce an installment of his series "Things I have learned in my life so far." This one minute clip about the importance of keeping a diary was shot in one day in an abandoned historic Tang Dynasty park.
Question & Answer on page 219

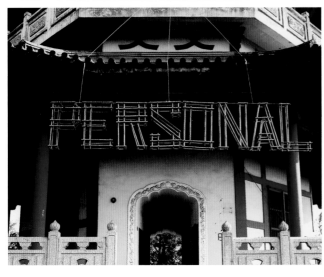

STEFAN SAGMEISTER

Underware held their type workshop at the Tampere Polytechnic School of Art and Media in Tampere, Finland. Participants were split into two groups, with one group making a thin typeface and the other a tiny one. The thin group's lettering was best-viewed from an aerial perspective.

Let it Run

The aim of Underware's type workshop held in Hanover, Germany, was to make type from dominos, spelling out: "type moves" (the theme of the Forum Typographie). Participants came up with very different approaches and at the end of the day all "stoppers" (gaps in the domino row) were removed very carefully and all of the individual "type moves" renderings were connected to create one, long domino effect. It was so long that it is actually recorded as the biggest type-domino ever created, using more than 13,000 single, hand-cut domino stones.

179

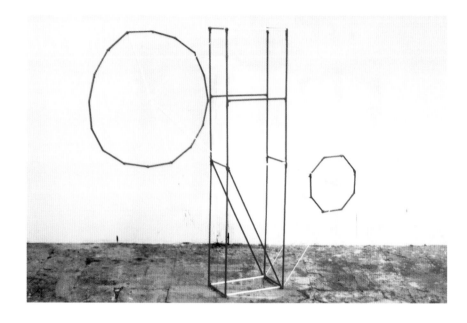

Oh No, Everything Must Glow,
and Not Much
(Clockwise from top)
Sculptor Nick van Woert's typographic sculptures have a spare,
structural quality reminscent
of scaffolds and large-scale advertising signage. The letterforms
are often built into the structure,
lending them an integrated,
architectural presence. Van Woert
lives and works in Brooklyn.

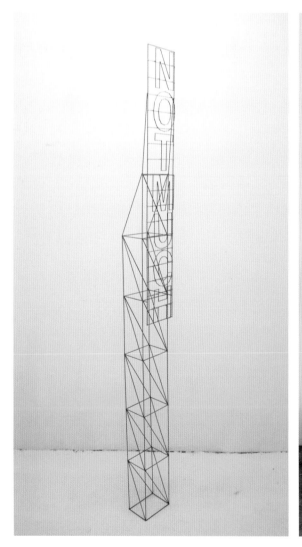

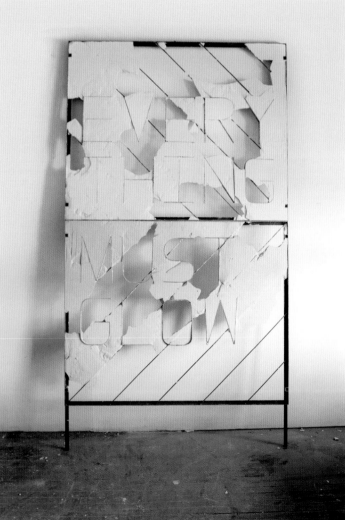

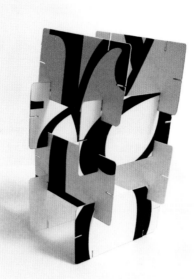

Visualization for a Staircase
Originally from Singapore, UK-based designer Huda Abdul Aziz's work focuses on typography, motion graphics, and branding. For her Visualization for a Staircase, Aziz created a dynamic display type; its legibility is dependent on the perspective from which it's read. This piece, along with her 3D visualization of a type sculpture, are examples of her interest in motion-based and deconstructed type. Both are prospective identity pieces for a fictional typographic museum called Type Factory, a project she explored during her senior year at University College Falmouth.

181

HUDA ABDUL AZIZ

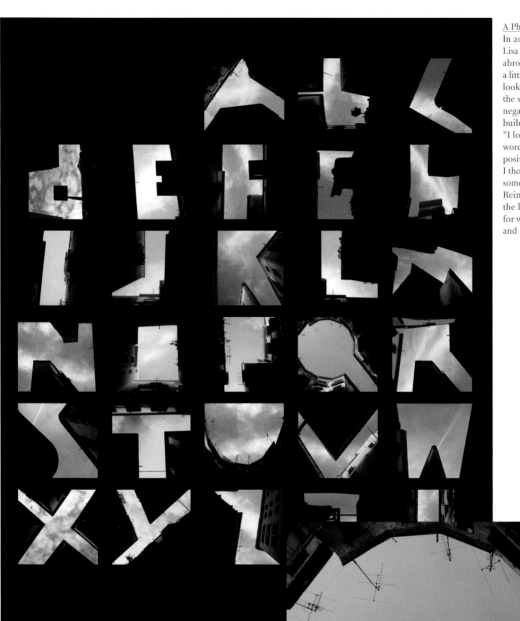

A Photographik Alphabet
In 2005, Berlin-based designer Lisa Reinermann spent a semester abroad in Spain. Standing in a little courtyard in Barcelona, she looked up and noticed houses, the sky, clouds, and a "Q." The negative space between the buildings formed the letter. "I loved the idea of the sky as words, the negative being the positive. If I could find a Q, I thought, other letters should be somewhere around the corner." Reinermann eventually found all the letters to complete the series for which she designed a book and fold-out poster.

LISA RIENERMANN   3D TYPOGRAPHY

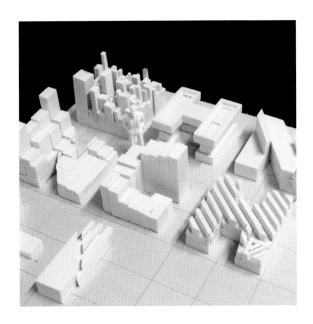

Shanghai World Expo
For an identity concept for the Shanghai World Expo 2010, Dutch designer John Beckers converted data about urban subsidence (the amount an area sinks into the ground) into a 3D infographic. The letterforms correlate to specific cities' subsidence data and are accompanied by booklets further explaining the numbers and raising awareness for global subsidence issues.

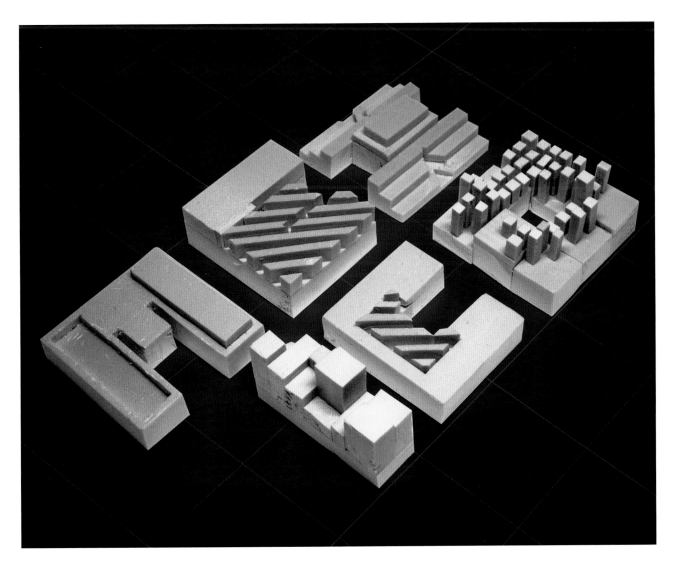

183

Porque las Palabras Están en Todas Partes / Porque as Palavras Estão por Toda Parte
(Because the words are everywhere)
For Porque las palabras están en todas partes, an installation for the exhibition "Proyectos para Deconstrucción," (Projects for Deconstruction) at MUCA Roma, México, and Galería Vermelho, São Paulo, Brazil, Brazilian artist Marilá Dardot constructed 33 concrete letters emerging from the floor. The letters compose the phrase "Porque las palabras están en todas partes," but can be read in a variety of combinations as one moves through the space. The Portuguese version of the work—"Porque as palavras estão por toda parte"—was produced for the artist's solo exhibition "Ficções," at Galeria Vermelho, São Paulo.

MARILÁ DARDOT

T
Danish designer Thorbjørn
Ankerstjerne was one of 26 designers,
invited to participate in YCN's
Alphabet project. Ankerstjerne was
assigned the letter "t." Because "t" is
the second most used consonant in
the English alphabet Ankerstjerne
wanted to be able to control its
visual presence. He achieved this by
alternating the letter's core to adjust
for boldness. T was made from a
wooden mold and epoxy.

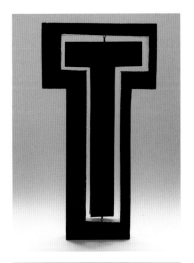

THORBJØRN ANKERSTJERNE

Utrecht Uitfeest Leidsche Rijn
Autobahn designed the 3D signage and typographic directionals for 25 artworks made for the Netherlands' Utrecht Uitfeest Leidsche Rijn, an event organized by the City of Utrecht and Beyond along with the permanent art program of Leidsche Rijn. Since the area is relatively new and unexplored, clearly visible signage, laser-cut from sustainable polystyrene, was required to allow visitors to navigate the grounds. In addition, Autobahn also designed the identity and promotional materials for the event, such as program booklets, flyers, posters, floor maps, banners, and a bicycle map, creating a cohesive visual experience.
Question & Answer on page 210

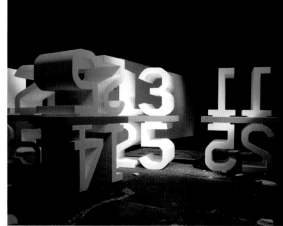

Inspired by conceptal artist Joseph Kosnuth's "One and Three Chair," New York City-based graphic designer Eric Ku explores the idea of re-definition through graphic design. "Instead of applying multiple definitions to the same chair, I redefined the structure of the chair by using typography," explains Ku. One is able to construct the chair by assembling the letters into a structural form.

187

HANS FINSLER

WERK – FOTOKLASSE –
MODERNE GESTALTUNG 1932–1966

UND DIE

SCHWEIZER

FOTO-

MUSEUM FÜR GESTALTUNG ZÜRICH
10.0 –17   2006

KULTUR

AUSSTELLUNGSSTRASSE 60
       ZÜRICH
       MUSEUM-GESTALTUNG.CH

Han Finsler Poster
Using shadow as a positive type
form, Swiss designers Kerstin
Landis, Naima Schalcher, and
Martina Walthert designed this
poster for an exhibition of the
photographer Hans Finsler's work
at the museum of design in Zurich.
The three designers studied
together at ZHdK Switzerland.

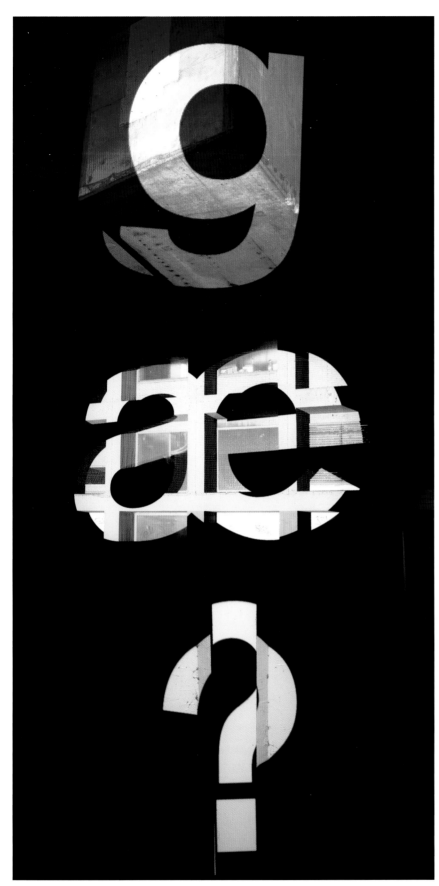

Tobias Battenberg is a sustainable graphic designer living and working in Cologne, Germany. For Akzidenz Grotesk Battenberg inserted the typeface—a sans-serif known for its resilience and character—into unexpected contexts. Using a video projector to beam type onto various buildings and objects in the city, Battenberg played with perspective, camera position, fracturing, and other special effects, paying special attention to the way the letters imposed their particular character onto the surface. The resulting photographed images are, as the name says, grotesque and miraculous.

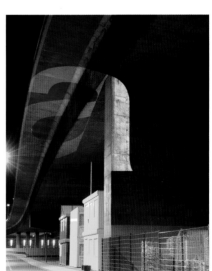

189

TOBIAS BATTENBERG

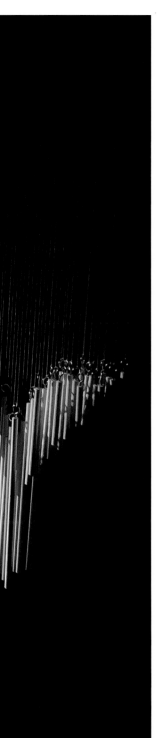

Agency

Oscar & Ewan is a small, London-based design studio working in a variety of mediums, including book design, music design, furniture design, and art installations. Oscar is from Stockholm, Sweden, and Ewan is from the Aberdeen, Scotland. For Agency, (opposite page) the designers created an organic and physical sign that responds to wind and movement. The letters are formed from individual, suspended sticks.

Discovery

For Metropolitan Works, London's first creative industries center, Oscar & Ewan were commissioned to do the exhibition design, from layout to printed materials. Because of the state-of-the-art digital manufacturing equipment available at Metropolitan Works, the designers were keen to use this technology and further showcase the center's facilities. Using a nylon rapid prototyping machine, the designers—with the help of 3D artist Chris Cornish—translated a simple 2D gradient into a 3D environment.

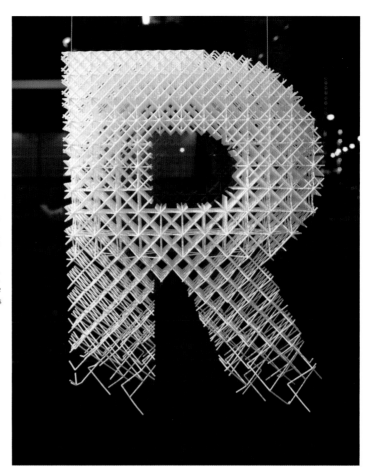

Obese and Cloak
Birmingham, UK-based James
Griffin is a graphic designer and
creator of the blog CMYKern.
For his experimental typefaces
Obese and Cloak he employed
material—cacti and black fabric,
respectively—to help create the
letterforms.

JAMES GRIFFIN

Jónas Valtýsson is a graphic designer living and working in Reykjavík, Iceland. For Sequences
Valtýsson collaborated with Siggi
Odds, Sven, and Mundi to create
a poster for an annual real-time art
festival hosted by the Living Arts
Museum in Reykjavík. For the
poster, the designers photographically captured milk in motion to
create type, hinting at the festival's
real-time focus. "We spent way
too much money buying many
liters of milk, but we had a lot of
fun while supplies lasted," says
Valtýsson. The posters were printed
in two-color offset, black and
a bright PMS 605, by an environ-
mentally-friendly printer.

After photographing a recent
Japanese ink calligraphy series, the
design team at Biwa Inc. attempted
to make Latin letters and English
words out of water suspended in
mid-air by strobe photography. "We
used P45 digital backs on Mamiya
Pro II D bodies, and Broncolor
Grafit A2 strobes to capture the images," explains Shinichi Maruyama,
photographer and creative director
of Biwa, Inc. "The strobes were the
most important asset, in that they
can capture motion and 'freeze' it
at 1/7500th of a second." Another
important aspect of the project was
patience, the patience to throw
liquid hundreds of times to get the
right shape and splash to get the
elements necessary to compose
the words. The shots were later
digitally composited in Photoshop,
though intersections, splashes,
and large pieces were all done in-
camera as much as possible.

195

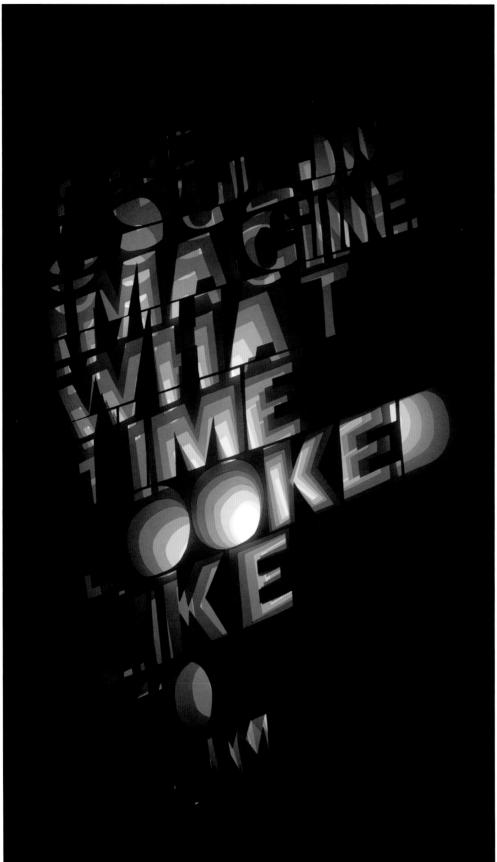

Untitled
This piece is part of a self-initiated project to typographically explore or enhance themes and concepts of visualizing time using quotations from the cult novel *Slaughterhouse Five* by Kurt Vonnegut. (Project continues on pages 36-37)

ALIDA ROSIE SAYER

Sick Helvetica

G&V is a multi-disciplinary visual collective producing conceptual work in the field of art direction, photography, and illustration. Founded in New York City by Swedish designer Gustaf von Arbin and French designer Vassili Brault, the duo challenges the border between art, fashion, and communication. For Sick Helvetica Arbin and Brault wanted to express the stigma and symptom of mental disease through a typeface considered to be universal in its (non) expression.

John Caserta is a designer and founder of The Design Office, an organization that supports independent designers in Providence, Rhode Island, where Caserta is also an adjunct faculty member at Rhode Island School of Design. Letterboxes is designed as a low-cost, interactive kids' toy. The 4-inch cubes may be viewed and stacked from any direction, creating unexpected shapes and letters. The boxes are made from recycled cardboard and delivered flat (assembling is part of the fun).

198

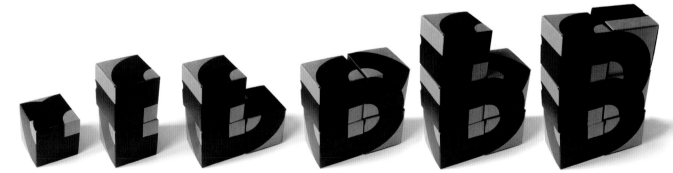

JOHN CASERTA

3D TYPOGRAPHY

Using the Rubik's Cube as a model, Liverpool-based graphic designer Jas Bhachu created a device that enables type design through re-combination: "I based the designs around three simple shapes: circles, triangles, and squares." The shapes were made out of rubber and adhered to the cube. The user can reconfigure the cube to create various letterforms.

199

JAS BHACHU

Graphic designers Per Emanuelsson and Bastian Bischoff founded Humans Since 1982 in 2008. The designers' Clock Clock font is based on projected clock hands on paper. The pointers follow a chromatic choreography that form letters intermittently. This concept is also applied to a wall clock, and a 24-hour manual alarm.

201

<u>Resevoir Dog</u>
Brussels-based Charles Mazé
created <u>Resevoir Dog</u> to design
large-scale type. Mazé created
a large stencil (in American Type-
writer) into which he unleashed
his mechanical drawing dog. The
battery-operated dog walks around
the stencil, coloring the blank
paper beneath. Each frame was
designed in order to use the small-
est number of elements (straight
lines made of wood, long and small
curves shaped in metal) allowing
the dog to color in each letter of
the alphabet. Mazé was commissioned to write the headline treatment for William Safire's "On
Language" column in the *The New
York Times*.

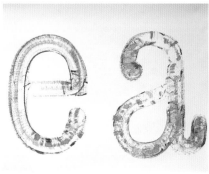

CHARLES MAZÉ

Morph

Miguel Ramirez is a Los Angeles-based designer. Through his studies at California State University, Long Beach, and Basel, Switzerland, and his work experience at Art Center College of Design, he has developed an interest in experimental typography. Morph highlights the transformation of cheese as it's grated into letters to form the word "nice."

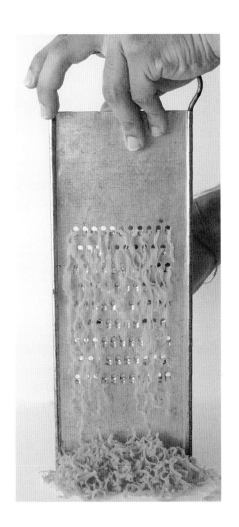

203

MIGUEL RAMIREZ

Time

British graphic designer David Marsh explored the concept of passing time by hand-molding candles into the shapes of letters and burning them. The resulting video and images illustrate the notion of time passing. A candle's association with birthdays also speaks to the idea of aging.

Stockholm-based Dutch designer Christiaan Postma assembled more than 150 individual clocks to form one clock. The time is spelled out from "one" to "twelve," with the words oriented clockwise. The word "three" appears when it's exactly 3 o'clock and will then transform again as time passes. The word "four" appears at exactly 4 o'clock, at which point the word "three" is by then totally vanished and no longer readable. Postma's "clock" was exhibited at Spazio Rossana Orlandi during the 2008 Milan Furniture Fair.

205

CHRISTIAAN POSTMA

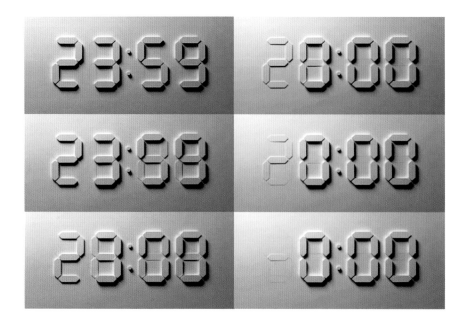

The mechanized segments of New York City-based designer Alvin Aronson's digital clock slowly protrude to reveal the current time. When a segment retracts it disappears seamlessly into the face of the clock. The slowly transitioning segments lend the clock a physical dimension as well as a fluid animated quality, resulting in an object that exists somewhere between the analog and digital realm.

206

Standard Time

Artist Mark Formanek emphasizes the meticulous, old-fashioned, and, above all, human experience of time. For the project, which was realized by Datenstrudel, 70 workers built a wooden 4 x 12 meter "digital" time display in real time. The work involved 1,611 changes within a 24-hour period. Seamlessly documented, the performance is now available on DVD, which includes software that synchronizes the movie to your computer clock.

DATENSTRUDEL / MARK FORMANEK

Chapter 6

Autobahn
Utrecht, NL

As a design studio working in a variety of mediums, what determines the appropriateness of 3D type for a project?
Every now and then we feel the urge to leave our computers and start making designs with our hands. Sometimes a blank paper and a lot of markers and pencils are sufficient, but other times we need tubes of toothpaste or pieces of old furniture to satisfy our creative needs. Since we all love typography and craft, an idea translates into 3D type quite easily. A lot of our clients are inspired by the fun and energy of these projects, which makes it easier to apply them to commissioned work.

How does the material inform the message or vice versa?
The funny thing about 3D type is that you look at [the form] and read [the letters] at the same time. It is important to understand those are two entirely different things. If one were to make the word "hard" out of pieces of rock, the image wouldn't be very exciting. Same goes for the word "soft" out of feathers. But when you invert that [relationship], something else happens. When the words and the materials are in dialogue, things become interesting. They don't need to reinforce each other, creating a contrast is probably more powerful.

Your Freshfont series—Heldentica (bottom), Gelvetica, Tomatica (top)—are all versions of Helvetica in liquid form. The resulting image is then photographed, redrawn, and made into a 2D useable typeface (available as a free, downloadable font). What was the inspiration for the Freshfont project? Have you seen the typeface used in other projects?
We were invited to present at a Pecha Kucha night in Amsterdam and were told to present twenty slides in twenty seconds. Most of the other speakers used the opportunity to present a short portfolio. We figured it would be more fun to do a new project instead. There wasn't actually a solid plan for the Heldentica, Gelvetica and Tomatica. We just experimented with all kinds of supermarket goods.

Many of your projects have collaborative themes and possess an air of adventure, is this a reflection of the atmostphere in the studio?
Yes, it is, actually! We like to tell the world that it is so much fun to have your own graphic design agency, to work hard and play hard, to do what you like to do. Adventurous design has a nice ring to it!

How is that important to your process?
In order to make the projects inspiring for us, they need to have a certain amount of risk. Is there enough time? What will it cost? Will the material hold? Taking risks moves you forward.

Where does your fascination with typography come from?
The fascination doesn't come from a single source. Maarten likes language and the way it evolves. Rob is more interested in the history and craftmanship of type. Jeroen is fascinated by the idea that modern typography enables him to add emotion to information; the letters read and tell a story on two different levels.

Projects on pages 55, 83, 157, 186

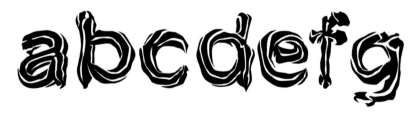

Andrew Byrom
Long Beach, California, US

What compells you to do so many letterform explorations in 3D? Do you feel limited by 2D typography?

I am interested in working with typographic form in 3D because it throws up new constraints that fundamentally shape the letterform.

Traditionally, typography is bound by the page. When type is taken from its printed form and presented as a 3D object, many historical conventions no longer seem applicable. For example, serifs have no structural meaning in 3D. In a physical space, architectural considerations need to be addressed. My work is not, for example, Helvetica rendered in 3D neon or steel, but rather is a reaction to the limitations of materials and processes that help shape or force the outcome of the design.

Where did the concept for the letterform kite project originate?

My Letter-Box-Kites (top) developed from an earlier "pop-up" signage system, Byrom-TSS. Each letter of Byrom-TSS stands about four feet tall and is fabricated from waterproof nylon wrapped around a fiberglass pole frame (see page 163).

I was exhibiting this design at a Design Within Reach event in Chicago, and as I was dismantling the type the wind picked up and the letters began to lift off down the street. A passerby asked if they were kites. They weren't, but I realized that with some reworking and a reduction in scale they very well could be.

It is unexpected to see blinds manipulated to make letterforms, but the the kineticism of your venetian blind type (bottom) is inspiring. What makes this project so unique?

The Venetian design is a departure for me because all of my other projects are designed and fabricated from scratch. With this project I am manipulating an existing object, which I think is a valid idea and has a striking effect. I have the feeling that Venetian is not finished and that its design will evolve into something else down the line.

How has growing up in Barrow, a shipbuilding town in the north of England, influenced your work?

I've never given this much thought, but it seems to make sense that my experiences working with my hands in the shipyard many years ago has affected how I approach my work today. Like generations of my family before me, I left school at sixteen and went to work in the local shipyard in Barrow. I worked there, serving an apprenticeship until I was twenty-one, at which point I left Barrow to go to art school and eventually to study in London.

Your low-cost temporary signage system fabricated from corrugated plastic suggests a relationship between typography and product design. Do you see a lot of crossover between the two disciplines?

I like the idea of creating objects that are useful. When designing traditional 2D typefaces you are basically creating tools for graphic designers, and the expected outcome and limitations are clear. My goal is to use typography to move into areas like product and furniture design. Here new sets of constraints inform the design choices. For example, with TSS-2 the overriding issue was to create a signage system that would be low-cost, light-weight, and be easily stored and shipped in a flat-package. After much exploration, corrugated plastic (with peel-off stickers) seemed to present itself as the best option.

Projects on pages 126–127, 160–163

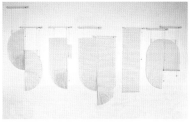

Atelier Pariri / Jerome Corgier
Paris, FR

What's the inspiration for your letterforms?
For Lara and me, inspiration comes from our diverse experiences and travels. (Lara Captan is my associate in Lebanon, with whom I collaborate.)

I am particularly interested in typography and the creation of characters. For example the work of Martin Venezky was, for me, a real revelation. He has a true liberty of creation and expression. As our work has progressed, I have tended to work more and more with volume, mixing typography and topology. An element of geography appeared early on in our work because maps are a source of inspiration for me.

Sometimes your letterforms begin as topographical drawings, which are then translated into 3D form. How do geology, topology, and architecture inform your work?
These are, indeed, very important elements in our work, simply because they create a unique language that is common to us both.

We use paper because it's malleable, easy to construct and deconstruct (few of our creations last a very long time), and it's lightweight. It allows us to realize our projects more easily.

Faceting, weaving, and layering paper often serve as a method for achieving volume in your letterforms. How do you approach creating a 3D form with a flat material?
It's precisely to give an extra dimension to the paper that I use it topologically, in layers. This way the volume increases rapidly. We took to this medium because of its ease of use, but we are going to move on to a different dimension. The paper letters are not just "models."

Your 3D letters have a singularity to them. What compels you to create such elaborate and ornate forms?
The character of our creations is not calculated in advance, but comes little by little, along with research and dialogue. The elements that compose our creations (paper, topology) accumulate along the way. Our language evolves little by little because it is the result of an exchange between two people from different cultures.

What are you working on currently?
At the moment Atelier Pariri is working to create letters that blend Arabic and Latin characters to form an alphabet. We would also like to put together small pedagogical volumes for children to teach the Arabic and Latin alphabets.
Projects on pages 14–17

212

Stephanie DeArmond
Minneapolis, Minnesota, US

Your work blurs the line between traditional pottery, sculpture, and signage. Embodying letterforms isn't common for ceramists. How did you progress from traditional ceramics toward working with typography?

I really enjoy making vessels, and that's still a part of my studio practice. I think it was through the process of making lots of pots and cups that I started to see them as frames for a drawing or a piece of text, which brought up their dual history as functional and decorative objects. I imagined reversing the hierarchy completely, whereby the text became the form upon which to apply decoration. My husband is a graphic designer, so over the years I've developed an awareness of typography via osmosis, particularly its ability to communicate different things through form, scale, and historical references. But in the end, I don't see a distinction between working with tableware or working with type forms.

Why is language important to your work?

Words have multiple levels of meaning, and I find letterforms to be fascinating formal objects. I want to create texts into which people can build their own meaning, or that give a new perspective on a familiar phrase or word. I like the idea of words losing their meaning through rhyme or repetition. I am interested in the way a phrase is transformed when it's transformed into a 3D object.

How do you go about choosing a typeface?

I'm always looking at signs out in the world, and I have a collection of old Dover typeface books that is a great resource for strange forms. Usually that's the starting point, and then I draw the letterforms freehand. When it comes to pairing a typeface with a piece of text, I look for something that adds to its meaning as a sculptural object. I like that these elements bring with them a specific decorative language, like old-timey, hip-hop, gothic, biblical, etc.

How did the commission for the "T" for *The New York Times T* Magazine come about?

They contacted me and asked me if I could do it! I'm not sure how they found me. I was so thrilled; I thought I was dreaming. And the art director had this amazing accent, which just added to the surrealism. I felt like I was going to call them up when it was ready to ship and they would say, "Who is this and why are you calling here?"

Why do you limit your color palette to white and neutrals and the decals?

I guess it was a process of eliminating all the glazes that I didn't like much and ending up with a super-neutral object. I wanted the surfaces to be appropriate for tableware but also to not soften the edges of the clay and diminish the beauty of the clay body. In this context, the decals helped to redefine the letterforms with something completely counter to the objects. Now I am rethinking that a bit; I want my current work to look like big pieces of candy!

Could you tell us more about your new work?

Until recently, our baby son has taken up most of my time, but now I have more opportunity to be in the studio, which is exciting. The three of us just returned from two years living in the Netherlands, and I am thinking about all of the things I saw there. I really love Dutch Golden Age painting and Delftware—historical European ceramics, in general. Also, in Holland, ceramics is understood in an industrial design context. It has made me think of the multiple differently. American ceramics takes much from the idea of the studio potter, whereas in Holland the norm for high-end pieces is that they are made by designers working collaboratively with small factories. Droog's work is very inspiring. In Holland, design and art come together to create wonderful collaborations, and ceramics is part of that; it is in dialogue with fashion, graphic design, and other areas.

For my new typographic pieces, I am working more with abstraction. It is more decorative and referential to French curves and cursive. There is less of a reference to signage and the forms are less readable. I am also working with tableware and taking care of my son, which is another big project.

Projects on pages 170–171

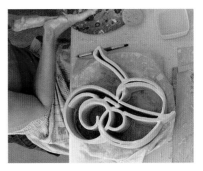
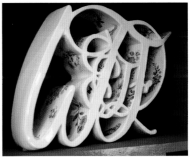

Oded Ezer
Givatayim, IL

As a designer working in a variety of mediums, what determines the appropriateness of 3D type for a project?
It always seemed to me that the 3D design of letters is a logical expansion of traditional 2D type design.

How did you start to work with 3D type?
Starting around 2000 I began investigating the possibilities of going one step further and "releasing" type from the 2D format. My intention is to create a surrounding that is both typographic and sensual. My starting point is to see myself as a typographer who creates sensations by combining materials, colors, and compositions in space.

You've said you love working with low-tech materials and simple ideas. How do you combine materials and messages?
Yes, I love working with low-tech materials, such as nails, glue, foam, silicone, etc. I also like simple ideas, non-complex execution, easy life. I think good design should be easy to perform, and I try to avoid the more complicated solutions.

As an Israeli designer you work with two languages, as well as two different alphabets. Do you feel limited by the forms of either alphabet?
I do believe that letters have enormous power in shaping our society and delivering messages and sensations. As an Israeli, my typographic culture is mainly based on traditional and contemporary Hebrew type systems. I am, of course, influenced by the cultural, national, and political environment of my country. I see myself obligated to question the borders of typographic design as they are in Israel and in other countries and to suggest alternative solutions.

A letter is both the content and the object that carries it. Is it a "thing" or a "symbol of a thing"—or both? I relate to these places because for me, when I make a hairy circle, it is a hairy circle. But if I write the word "circle" in a hairy way, it opens up a whole new field for interpretation. This is why I'm a typographer. I love hating the letters; I love loving them; I can betray them or be loyal to them.

Your projects feel as though they have a life of their own. What's your inspiration when developing your letterforms' life force?
In my Biotypography project, I have manipulated Hebrew and Latin characters to make "typo creatures." The project's name comes from my idea of a typography based on biology. "Biotypography" is any typographical application that uses biological systems, living organisms, or derivatives thereof, to create or modify typographical phenomena.

These small typo creatures are made of black polymer clay ("Fimo"), black sponge, and plastic. I had hoped to create live, almost cinematic situations where these typo creatures could act. The most difficult thing while working on the project was the "balance"—where to draw the line between the insect and the letter, how recognizable should the ant be and how readable should the letter be? It took me some time to understand that I don't really need the whole ant to make my point... and that the letter doesn't necessarily have to be complete.

When did you develop an interest in type?
Since early childhood, I've been fascinated by letters and typography. I studied every street sign and magazine trying to understand why type looks the way it looks. I printed newspapers with my friends while still in elementary school, designing page layouts at the age of ten. At twenty-two, I went to study graphic design and typography in the academy.

What's next?
The definition of a typographer is outdated. I don't see myself as a scientist or an artist, just as a typographer who wants to break barriers. My goal is to figure out what can be done with letters that has never been done before. I want my thinking to become even more elastic. For future projects, I will experiment with masks as well as with languages like Arabic, Farsi, and Japanese.
Projects on pages 26—27, 148—149

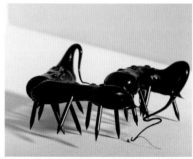

Anna Garforth
London, UK

In your "Moss" series, the relationship between the text, material, and location seems very much intertwined. How do you select the location for these pieces? How does the location influence the text?

Moss is usually already growing in a place where we have sited a piece. It was not so much the specific location that influenced the text, but rather past experiences, poetry (by Eleanor Stevens) and simple words that say a lot.

Can you describe the process of working with a live material?

The best thing about working with a natural material is where it takes you. I am no longer bound to my studio during the creative process, I find myself outside a lot of the time exploring the more wild parts of the city, foraging for inspiration and materials. It has also led me to delve into new interests such as bee keeping and sustainable architecture. The patterns in nature's design have always inspired me. One day I decided I wanted to work with more than a pen and a flat piece of paper, so I went out for the day, collected moss, leaves, and other things and started experimenting. My ideas come from working, crafting, and understanding the material and its qualities.

Where is your next moss installation?

The moss art is taking a back seat for a while, and I am currently developing many new ideas that I hope to test out on the public soon! I am currently experimenting with natural media such as, birch bark, nettle leaves, and lichen.

For Trash Type, you collected rubbish to create the letterforms to spell "used"? This is a clear instance of the medium informing the message; can you describe how you arrived at this process?

This was a great project; we got really excited about rummaging for rubbish! We couldn't go past a bin without taking a second glance; our eyes became attuned to finding colorful crisp packets, polystyrene cups, cardboard, and any general rubbish that could be rolled. It took a while for the students to get involved, but when they did, they loved it! The rubbish found new value and was seen as a material that could be re-used. We spent hours in piles of plastic packaging rolling the rubbish into tight tubes and packing them together, creating the word "used." The relationship between message and medium is a clear one: reduce, re-use, recycle.

Where does your fascination with typography come from?

I am from an illustration background and have always struggled with typography. Being inspired by graphic designers such as Stefan Sagmeister, I started to see type as being more pictorial and less literal. My interest in type is a recent one, and I am now aiming to marry my illustration skills with my new-found enthusiasm for letterform.
Projects on pages 78–79, 110–111

Gyöngy Laky
San Francisco, California, US

Your work blurs the boundary between traditional textile, sculpture, and signage. How did you shift from producing traditional textiles to working with typography?
Being a sculptor, I have always preferred 3D work with physical presence that uses space and interacts with the surroundings. When I think about the symbolic life force of letters and words, I visualize them as sculptural forms. I consider symbols to be language and often find them more enigmatic and fascinating than a complete word.

My weaving quickly became an effort to use the loom to make dimensional sculpture. I abandoned weaving in the late 1970s, finding semi-rigid materials and rope much more conducive to defying gravity.

Why is language important to your work?
I have always had an affinity for both visual arts and 3D form, and I suspect that I looked at letters like shapes, especially while trying to learn how to read and speak a new language. My fluency with languages was established early on. I learned to speak both Hungarian and German as all Hungarians spoke both at that time. My mother's native tongue, however, was Polish, and I am sure she spoke Polish to me as a baby. (She was also fluent in French and spoke that with her mother.) My father, on the other hand, went to college in the US, and I am certain he wanted to speak English all of the time! This suggests that I was exposed to four—maybe five—languages prior to age five.

How do you go about choosing a typeface for your letterforms?
My words and letters have been mostly simple capital block style. The lettering for my war works came from letters I found in the newspaper.

What's your fascination with ampersands?
In my language works, I've borrowed from the ideas of the concrete poets and their visual poetry—that physical attributes, patterns, and arrangements have the potential to enhance meaning. 3D letters have always been extremely satisfying to me. The specific choices I make in selecting materials and structuring form allows me to experiment with intent and attitude, extending and altering the possible interpretation.

When I was on the faculty at UC Davis in the mid-90s, one of my students had some level of dyslexia that was quite pronounced in certain areas of her activity such as language usage. I was fascinated by a story she told me of a time when she made great progress in this particular area. She had difficulty using, spelling, understanding, and writing multisyllabic words. She began to form these larger words by making the letters three-dimensionally out of clay. As she formed each dimensional word she was able to make it her own!

For me, the ampersand conveys connection, continuation, relationship, more, interdependence, history, past and present, partnership, inclusion, expectation, and much more. It is often a place-holder, a thought-gathering device.

Do you feel limited by the forms of the alphabet? Would you like to make new letterforms? What would your 27th character look like?
Some of my abstract linear wall works in the 1980s and 90s made me think that I was creating calligraphic/runic/pictographic forms. I recently completed a small wire bowl that I titled "Runic Reading" so I may be heading back toward creating my own illegible letterforms.

What's next?
I am now beginning work on a blood red question mark littered with small, black, plastic GI Joes. I found this question mark high on a building in San Francisco's Chinatown recently.

I would like to do numbers, but they are not coming readily. And I would like to do some other symbols like mathematical notation. I have been working on Chinese characters, but, again, they are difficult and I am still waiting for them to come out. The Yuan was easy; it is such a beautiful form.
Projects on pages 72—75

216

Clotilde Olyff
Brussels, BE

How did you arrive at the idea for the Pebble Alphabets (top) project?
During 1999's summer vacation I found some pebbles on the beach that were in the shape of letters. I told myself that maybe one day I could find a whole alphabet. At the end of summer (October of that year), I had decided that the theme for my dissertation would be the idea of a type foundry that would show letters from different angles. After four stays by the sea during that time, I was able to complete my first alphabet.

How many hours did you comb the beaches of Les Landes, searching for your various alphabet families? What was your selection process? Do you search for a letter or do you have the letter find you?
I calculate in years—20 years! There was a two-year interruption after an oil tanker sank into the sea on the north of Spain and polluted all of France's southwest beaches. The beaches were cleaned so thoroughly that there weren't any pebbles left. I was unemployed! Now they are back. But while I waited, I discovered the little pieces of wood, and the rubbish in the shape of letters brought by the sea.

The pebbles are like wine: there are good years and there are bad years, depending on the mood of the Atlantic. I find them on three French beaches, 1,000 km from my home in Brussels. If I go too far north of the first beach or too south of the third, I don't find any. In the beginning, I used the palm of my hand to measure of height for the letters. Then when I realized there were too many, I started picking up all of those that loosely resembled letters. I now divide them into little bags in my cabinets. Once in a while, I pull them all out and compose alphabets—to this day more then 30 alphabets exist (upper case, lower case, numbers, and punctuation).

Where does your fascination with typography come from?
I was born into it because my dad was a typographer and a graphic designer. And also because I am dyslexic. When you have dyslexia there are two options, you can either run from it or dive into it. If you love the letter,

you will one day maybe be able to love the word, the phrase, and who knows... the whole text! To read and to write is a big adventure for a dyslexic!

Why do many of your explorations result in 3D letterforms?
I started with 2D: I drew a lot of alphabets, always on paper. From that I discovered the form of the letter, the "game" of the letter, of its construction. But it wasn't until I could touch it, feel its matter, its weight, and once I could manipulate it that I found a new relation with it—something more emotional.

Why have you created so many games/puzzles about the construction of letterforms?
All of my childhood was spent seeing speech therapists. They always made me play with patterns made of cars, houses, birds, flowers, etc. Never with the letters. So since I work with the drawing of the letter, its construction in 2D and 3D, it seemed a logical step to approach the typographical game. I love the object. I love constructing the letter in 3D. A game is very different then a sculpture: one moves, the other is fixed... for now!

Is there a belief system or philosophy that drives your thinking when creating letterforms and games?
Have fun!

Why did the letter "A" feel the need to give the "e" an attitude adjustment?
Emotion moves us through different states, so in the face of fear, in function of the design of the letter we move from the "c" (full) to the "e" (with it's big mouth) to return to the "c" (which is only mouth).

What are you currently working on?
A collection of books based on fonts and icons. There are 62 different books—36 of these are part of a collection (a book per number and a book per letter), 16 are their own books and the rest are special editions. I create, produce, and edit them.
Projects on pages 76–77, 125

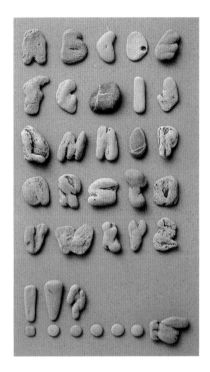

Camilo Rojas
Miami, Florida, US

In your Enjoy, Flavor, and Gold pieces brand messages are manipulated to expose the way in which marketing masks the negative effects of consuming certain products. How did you conceive of these projects?

This project was born out of the need I had to expose audiences to social problems, concepts, and ideals through the power of typography. I could communicate and represent outside of the usual screen-and-print-based forms. "Consumption," was created during my senior year at New World School of the Arts. It took me approximately six months to complete.

Enjoy, Flavor, and Gold criticize specific brands to expose the dangers of their widely-consumed products. The aim is to teach and bring attention to these problems.

I attempted to keep the pieces very honest and realistic. The dark silver background in Flavor was created using cigarette ashes, which helps to make the piece smell stronger; the nails in Enjoy were corroded by Coca-Cola. I wanted to awaken the audience's senses and create a stronger connection between the viewer and the work. I believed that a shock factor, like looking closer at the nicotine in the cigarettes or seeing that Coke can actually corrode a nail, will strongly impact the audience.

Where did you get 3,000 half-smoked cigarettes to create the word "flavor"?

I thought this piece was never going to see the light of day because of the high cost of cigarettes. I started by collecting cigarette butts from the streets, friends, anywhere I could find them. After a lot of tests and experiments I realized this method did not work as planned; it would take me months before I collected all of the cigarettes I needed. Plus, most of the cigarettes I got were really damaged and in bad shape and did not have the right size or the filter didn't have the color I needed. I decided then to buy the cartons of cigarettes and smoke the cigarettes myself, but it was not working. After a couple experiments, I ended up vacuuming tips of the filters; this absorbed more nicotine and it achieved the right color and more control over the size.

Where does your fascination with letters come from?

My fascination with typography started when I was little. I remember ever since I was in the fourth grade drawing letters, personal names, and band names all over my notebooks. I believe my attraction to letters comes from my urge to look beyond screens and I've been developing that need by investigating new materials and unconventional processes to innovate typography's endless forms. I have a huge desire to challenge traditional limitations, to play, experiment, and push the traditional typographic boundaries.

What's next?

My biggest desire is to stop moving from one idea to another and really start turning them into a reality. I want to set goals and move my ideas forward. Additionally, by using my passion for design as a tool I would like to create awareness and help solve problems that effect our society and the world in general in a way that entertains and embraces people through positive change. This is a work in progress; I actually still think I could help change the world... help humanity move toward a more simple, happy, peaceful, playful, creative, and sustainable existence.

Projects on pages 68, 154−155

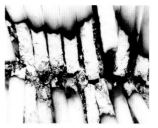

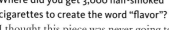

Stefan Sagmeister
New York, New York, US

Your grandfather was a sign painter. Did his work influence you?

Yes. I grew up with his ornamental wood signs all over our apartment.

You're well-known for creating your own type to craft a message. What do you gain by this approach?

So much of the work that is created by professional designers leaves me cold. Using hand lettering and a more humanistic approach constitutes an attempt to bring a more personal point of view to the viewer.

At the TED Conference your presentation was entitled "Yes Design Can Make You Happy." Does creating messages in 3D make you happy?

3D does not create happiness. Dealing with content that I am truly interested in and care about, however, does.

Your work is both humorous and serious at the same time. What is your belief system or philosophy toward making work?

I believe that in certain circumstances design can touch viewers' hearts. This can be achieved through humor and seriousness.

What was the impetus for your Worrying Solves Nothing piece?

I used to lie awake at night brooding over problems that came up during the day. It kept me from sleeping. It was not enjoyable, and most importantly, I never arrived at a solution for anything—a remarkably effective way to be miserable. So I stopped. I now actively try to get my mind to concentrate on something else when I go to sleep. When my daytime worrying gets bad, I try to envision the worst-case scenario: What is absolutely the most terrible outcome possible? This often turns out to be the loss of a client or some other professional setback, which, when I think about it for a second, is not that tragic after all.

We created the saying for the OK Centrum in Linz. Austrian school kids built the maxim out of 25,000 black and 35,000 white cloth hangers. Four hangers were bound together with wire fasteners to form a square; six of these completed squares formed a cube; the cubes, in turn, formed pixels. Each letter stands about ten feet (three meters) high, with the entire sentence configuring a 125-foot-long (38 meters) block, a lacy typographic sculpture placed parallel to the building's facade on the Spittelwiese, a pedestrian zone in the center of Linz.

Tell us more about the Singapore commercial?

We were invited to Singapore to produce another installment of the series "Things I have learned in my life so far." This one minute clip about the importance of keeping a diary was shot in one day in an abandoned historic Tang Dynasty park in Singapore.

Projects on pages 102–105, 177

219

Dan Tobin Smith
London, UK

You are a photographer. Where did your interest in typography arise?

I've always been interested in typography as a form of design, and I like the idea of photographically representing typography.

Aesthetically letters are interesting forms, especially when they are represented photographically.

Do you have typefaces in mind before you begin crafting your letterforms or do you craft each letterform spontaneously?

I base my letterforms on Helvetica. It normally ends up being slightly bolder than usual, just because of the nature of the photographic process. It's a design classic and I wanted to stick with one font as changing the font between images changes the rules of the shoot and I wanted some things like the format of the image and the ratios of the represented letters to remain consistent. This way it's more about the content.

Your sets seem elaborate and precise. How do you plan for your shots?

A lot of the sets start in my head. I have a good idea of what is going to work from experience of shooting a lot of similar still-life pieces. It's also a little bit of trial and error on the day of the shoot. Depending on the size of the set it usually takes a few days to build and shoot. I've also worked with the set designer Nicola Yeoman on a couple projects.

You're currently creating an entire alphabet (bottom). How is that process going?

Slowly! I've shot six so far and have two more in pre-production. It will take a few years!

Are you shooting the letters for the alphabet project in alphabetic order or are you working with your favorite characters first?

The process is not alphabetical order or based on favorite letters; it's quite random. Some are chosen because they work with the visual idea for the photograph.

What are you currently working on?

I am working on a few more letters and the usual mix of editorial work for people like *Wallpaper** magazine and advertising briefs. Also shooting and finishing the retouch on a number of personal projects, which I hope to exhibit next year. I will be launching a little website for the alphabet series in the new year which will grow nice and slowly! Projects on pages 140—141

220

Typeworkshop /Underware
Den Haag & Amsterdam, NL; Helsinki, FI

Where and when did you teach your first workshop?

It was in 2000 in Lahti, Finland. Our workshop was part of the HelveticaTimesExtraBold conference, which is a type event organized by Ritu Leinonen from the Lahti Polytechnic School of Art & Media. Soon after this a workshop on interactive videoclips followed at the UIAH in Helsinki. It may seem that we do these workshops full time, but that's not the case. We didn't really plan this in advance, it more or less just happened. We got more attention for doing these workshops when we made a website for a two-week workshop in October 2002; it was a combined workshop between the two art academies of Lahti & Helsinki. Our idea behind the website was bringing the students in contact with people outside the academy. By giving other people the opportunity to react to what students created, participants of the workshop got extra stimulated. Before continuing the workshop in the morning, these reactions were read by the participants and influenced the process in a nice way. This way participants got in contact with professionals (and non-professionals) with whom they might never have been in touch with otherwise.

We decided to make a website for every workshop, updating the site daily while the workshop is in session. By doing this, we created a site that shows a collection of research and experiments in type design. We also included a collection of links to other places on the web, so it's a fairly handy resource for someone who is totally new to the field of type design.

What is your intention with these workshops?

Sharing knowledge and the pleasure of creating something with a group of people. The traditional master-student approach is not our approach. We can learn as much from our students as they can learn from us. But of course, on certain topics we have some knowledge they don't have, and we are happy to share this knowledge.

What do you teach the students?

It depends on the amount of time. A four-day workshop is somethinwg different than a two-week workshop. Type design is a long and slow process, at least in the way we do it. It's not realistic to create a whole new typeface in only one week. It's more realistic to find the right approach in solving one typographic problem. For example, during the Thin & Tiny Type workshop in Tampere, a font called Nuts was the result of the tiny group. They examined the essential aspects of a typeface meant to be printed in extremely small sizes. The final font is not finished, or complete or perfect, but it does possess some of the essential elements. We encourage people to work together on one typeface; dividing the labor makes it more realistic to achieve a satisfying result, and cooperating in a group creates the opportunity to learn a lot from one another.

Most participants don't have a clear grasp of type design. We see this as a big advantage. Rigid and rigorous decisions are made more easily if one isn't limited by convention. Of course, it's useful to be aware of tradition. Having a thorough knowledge of a certain subject creates new possibilities.

Why do you choose to work with 3D type during the workshops?

If you look carefully, you will also see lots of classy 2D stuff. In fact we often start by sketching on paper. We do not have one standard way to run a workshop. To keep them interesting for ourselves and for participants, we always look for new concepts and ideas. Then, the typographic tools are based on that idea. So, we do not define a tool (pencil, snow, bricks, cardboard, brush, shopping carts, etc.) in advance—it's up to the participants to decide which tools work best to fulfill their ideas.

Projects on pages 50–51, 128–129, 178–179

221

Contributors List

Photo Credits

p. 6
Let'em Eat Cake and The Industrial
Complex/ Photo by M—36
Spiritual Revolutionary: Lenore
Tawney / Photo by Laurie Frankel

p. 39
Lectures dans la ville /
Photos by Sophie Huguenot

p. 52
Rubies Record Cover /
Photos by Danielle Rubi

p. 58
Twilight, Gravity, and Our Many
Impossible Things /
Photos by Tatsuro Nishimura

p. 72
GO And,... and Estuary /
Photos by Ben Blackwell
Negative /
Photo by M. Lee Fatherree

p. 73
Lakey in her studio /
Photo by Melissa Sachs
Domain Change /
Photo by M. Lee Fatherree

p.74
Give and Take /
Photo by Bob Hsiang

p.75
Longing For Tomorrow /
Photo by Bob Hsiang

p.82
A Origem da Obra de Arte
(top right) /
Photo by Eduardo Eckenfels
A Origem da Obra de Arte /
Photo by Matheus Rocha Pitta

p.83
Explorers /
Photo by Marieke Wijntjes

p.88
Eyelash typeface /
Photos by Kaile Hart

p.91
Typeface in Skin /
Photos by Arjan Benning

p. 102, 103
Obsessions Make My Life
Worse and My Work Better /
Photos by Jens Rehr

p.104, 105
Having / guts / always /
works out/ for / me /
Photos by Bela Borsodi

p. 148
Unimportant & Nothing /
Photo by Shaxaf Haber

p. 169
Signature vases /
Photo by Droog

p. 184
Porque las palabras están
en todas partes /
Photos by Ding Musa

p. 200
clock clock /
Photo by Christoffer T. Duff

p. 214
Rooms /
Photo by Idan Gil

p. 219
Worrying solves Nothing, Linz /
Photo by Otto Saxinger

Acknowledgements
The authors would like to thank
our contributors; Mike Abbink,
Joe Avery, American Craft Council,
Deborah Bishop, Amber Bravo,
Karrie Jacobs, Junko Kitano,
Yasuhiro Mizoi, Scott Newlin,
Lisa Paclet, Mike Perry, Andrew
Sawyer and Andrew Wagner for
their encouragement and support
—without them this project
would not have been possible.

About the Authors
Jeanette Abbink opened the design
studio Rational Beauty in 2008.
Prior to opening Rational Beauty,
Abbink was the founding creative
director of *Dwell* magazine. She
has also served as a designer
and art director for numerous
magazines, including *The New
York Times* sports magazine *Play,*
as well as *American Craft* and
Martha Stewart Living.

Graphic designer Emily CM
Anderson was selected as an
Art Directors Club Young Gun
6 in 2008. She has worked for
magazines such as *Dwell* and
American Craft, and co-designed
the book *Brooklyn Modern*
for Rizzoli.

224